The Shayer Family of Painters

The Shayer Family of Painters

Brian Stewart and Mervyn Cutten

F. Lewis, Publishers · London

First published 1981
by F. Lewis, Publishers, Limited
35 Bedford Row, London WC1R 4JH

ISBN 0-85317-092-4

Stewart, Brian
The Shayer family of painters.
1. Shayer *(Family)*
I. Title   II. Cutten, Mervyn
759.2   ND497.S451
ISBN 0-85317-092-4

Filmset by August Filmsetting, Stockport, Cheshire
Printed and bound in Great Britain
at The Pitman Press, Bath

Contents

List of Illustrations

Colour Plates

Black and White Illustrations within Text

Black and White Plates

WILLIAM SHAYER

Acknowledgements

In preparing this book the authors sought advice and assistance from many people, and the kindness and enthusiasm with which our enquiries were answered gave us considerable encouragement.

Particular thanks are due to Colin Dudley, Head of Art at Christ Church College, Canterbury, and to Mary Anne Stevens of Kent University, for offering their learned and perceptive advice throughout the entire production of this book.

Mr and Mrs Patrick Combes, Mr and Mrs Denis Combes, and Anthony Combes (all descendants of Shayer's brother-in-law William Combes) gave us the benefit of their knowledge generously supported by the provision of delicious teas, while Bernard Price kindly wrote the foreword in addition to providing us with a great deal of encouragement.

We would like to thank Dr John Barrell for his help with 'the rural poor', Roger Smith for his help with the section dealing with the Art Unions, Keith Lovet Watson for his information on the historical background, particularly with regard to the Press Gangs, Jan Reynolds for her invaluable advice on many practical matters, and to Stephen Sartin for his help and inspiration.

Thanks must also go to all those auction houses and galleries that assisted us with our enquiries, particularly those mentioned in the catalogue and those acknowledged in the plates. In this respect special thanks are due to Mr I. R. D. Byfield of the Richard Green Gallery and Margie Christian of Christie, Manson and Woods, whose generosity and efficiency added considerably to the ease and pleasure of our task.

We are grateful for the kind assistance of the following:
Mr John Appleby, Mr E. H. H. Archibald, Mr S. Balldock, Mr B. Bellinger, Mr M. Berry, Mr A. H. Brand, Mr D. Brittain, Group Capt. & Mrs G. Bryer, Mr L. Buckingham, Mrs H. Chaundy, Mrs J. Clarke, Mr Ross Collier, Miss Julia Collieu, Mr John H. Cooling, Miss Peggy Culver, Mrs Daphne Cutten, Mr Harold Day, Miss Liz-Anne Deeks, Mr Trevor Fawcett, Mr David Fuller, Mr Roger Freer, Mrs Patricia Gill, Miss Helen Guiterman, Mr Robin Hamlyn, Mr J. P. Hammond, Mr R. Harmer, Mr B. G. Hart, Mr F. Hatt, Mr F. Hills, Miss A. Hook and her family, Mr B. Ingram, Mrs B. Isaacs, Mr Bob Jack, Miss Gay Johnson, Mr Peter Johnson, Mr Lionel Lambourne, Mr Jeremy Maas, Mr John Marshall, Miss Ann Mathie, Mr Peter McCulloch, Mr David Messum, Mr and Mrs Moody, Mr P. R. Moston, Mr John Munday, Mr N. R. Omell, Miss Constance Anne Parker, Mr L. Paton, Mr Paul 'Wally' Reading, Mr and Mrs K. Sibley, Mr F. Simpson, Mr Ian Stewart, Dr and Mrs V. O. Stewart, Mr J. Sunderland, Dr Raymond Turley, Mr S. W. Wade, Ms Stella Walker, Mr Pete Wakelin, Mrs Marylian Watney, Miss Valerie Winn, Mr Christopher Wood, Ms Monica Woodhouse, Mrs R. Wooldridge, the Record Offices of the Isle of Wight, Portsmouth, Southampton, West Sussex and Winchester, the National Science

Museum, the Southampton Library and Archive, the Tate Gallery Archive, Portsmouth Library, Chichester Library, Christ Church Library, Canterbury, the Witt Library, the Paul Mellon Centre for British Art, the Yale Centre for British Art, the Society of Genealogists and the *Southern Evening Echo*.

Our expression of sincere gratitude to so many who have assisted us in our labour would be incomplete without the mention of both Mrs Joan Linnel Burton whose kindness led unexpectedly to the writing of this book, and to Mr Richard Green for most generously helping to finance the printing of the colour plates.

Foreword

I have been interested in the landscape of Britain and in the artists who have portrayed it in paint and pencil for as long as I can remember, and having been born in Sussex it was inevitable that I became aware of William Shayer and his work at an early stage. Shayer and his sons had succeeded in capturing the image and spirit of rural and coastal life in central southern England during the nineteenth century with great skill. Indeed, much of the painting seemed to me to be not only competent, but of a very high order. In the years immediately following World War II many fine works by William Shayer senior appeared on the art market but, not then being widely regarded as a fashionable painter, the quality of his work was frequently overlooked by buyers in favour of other names, and few works of reference paid more than scant attention to Shayer senior or his family.

It was Colonel Maurice Grant who, in his excellent volume *The Old English Landscape Painters* commented of Shayer: 'Of him little is known but his works, which are so numerous and so uniformly excellent as to render his biographical obscurity a matter of regret'. Well, in this volume the authors, Brian Stewart and my old friend Mervyn Cutten, whose family once employed Shayer as a coachpainter, have done much to redress the balance. Their research over many years has yielded an important and fascinating harvest of information that illuminates the Shayer family for the first time, and with the clarity of rich light that is to be found in so many of the landscapes themselves. There is, undoubtedly, more to be learned of this highly talented family, but this book will, I believe, provide the springboard for all future studies. Proof of the need for a book such as this arrives on my desk almost weekly in the form of catalogues attributing paintings to 'Shayer'. The photographs that have been so carefully selected for this work will certainly help in solving many of the problems of demarcation that exist between Shayer senior, his sons, and many followers. Such illustrations are particularly welcome when considering his many near duplicate works with their subtle variations, and Brian Stewart draws our attention to the possibility of 'pouncing' techniques having been used from time to time.

William Shayer had an exceptional eye for composition and handled his subjects with an admirable blend of controlled technique and imagination. The landscape that he most made his own was the New Forest; the woodland glades, gypsy camps, their characters and animals, all are portrayed with perception, sympathy and humour. The quality of such work was not lost upon his fellow painters, but Shayer doggedly resisted all encouragement to pursue his career in London. His Hampshire landscapes beckoned more beguilingly than those of the city and, with his pictures in popular demand, he clearly felt no need to disturb his roots. This may well be the reason for his dwelling in the background of British painting for so long; the emergence of Shayer and his heirs through this book can only lead to increasing recognition and appreciation of their true stature, and this is not only welcome but long overdue.

BERNARD PRICE

Abbreviations

B.I.	The British Institution, London
H.P.G.	The Hampshire Picture Gallery, Southampton
L.A.	The Liverpool Academy
R.A.	The Royal Academy of Arts, London
R.B.S.A.	The Royal Birmingham Society of Artists
R.G.I.F.A.	The Royal Glasgow Institute of Fine Arts
R.M.I.	The Royal Manchester Institution
S.B.A.	The Society of British Artists
W.S.A.F.A.	The West Scotland Academy of Fine Arts
A.U.P.	Art Union Prize
bt.	bought
bt. pt. A.U.P.	bought partly with an Art Union Prize, to which the winner added his own money.
Engraved	certain works chosen by Art Union prizewinners were engraved. However, these were of very poor quality, serving merely as mementoes. They were extremely small and each plate issued contained as many as seven paintings by various artists fortunate enough to have their work selected by Art Union prizewinners. See the *London Art Union Prize Annual*, 1845–8, by R. A. Sprigg.
fl.	flourished
*	information gleaned from periodicals that might help to identify a work.
w.c.	water colour

CHAPTER ONE
William Shayer 1787–1879

Biography

Comparatively little is known of William Shayer's early life. He was from relatively humble origins, his father Joseph being the publican of the Turk's Head in Spring Gardens, Southampton, whilst his mother Elizabeth was the daughter of John Ayling, a Chichester barber. William was baptised in St. Mary's Church on 14th June 1787, and so was not born in 1788 as is often stated. As Joseph was occupying the Turk's Head during this period it seems probable that it was here that the artist was born.

Towards the latter half of 1788 the Shayer family moved to the larger and presumably more profitable premises of the Horse and Jockey, which was situated in East Street at the corner of Canal Walk in Southampton. The rent was twenty-five pounds per annum, which was no small sum for the period, but to help meet this cost Joseph found it convenient to let part of the property to a blacksmith.

William's childhood cannot have been easy. In 1792, when the artist was five years old, his father died leaving Elizabeth to run the Horse and Jockey and to bring up William, his elder sister Charlotte, and two younger brothers John and George. Two years later in 1794, within the short space of a fortnight, both of his younger brothers died, probably from the result of an infectious disease. Naturally, under such difficult circumstances, William would have assisted his mother with the many chores involved in running a public house and, in so doing, must have accumulated considerable knowledge of the publican's trade. Surprisingly, instead of continuing the family trade, he took employment as an ornamental furniture painter, enhancing 'rush bottom chairs' with his elaborate decorations, and it must be assumed, therefore, that from an early age he showed considerable artistic talent.

By about 1801 or 1802 his work as a furniture painter had led him to embark upon an apprenticeship to a coachpainter, although the decision to do so may not have been wholly a matter of artistic commitment. The Napoleonic Wars were being fought and Press Gangs were searching streets and taverns, even houses, for able-bodied men to serve in the British Navy. One favourite method of 'recruitment' was to wait outside a church during a marriage service and catch the bridegroom and his friends as they emerged. Once caught, these unfortunate men would be put in a sea-going vessel, where they would remain until the crew was paid off, possibly six or seven years later, although in wartime even this release was unlikely. Officially, the Press was not allowed to take apprentices but this rule was seldom, if ever, observed. As the Horse and Jockey was frequented mainly by seafolk William would have been at some risk had he remained. It would be, therefore, a wise decision to move inland for apprenticeship.

THE COACHPAINTING APPRENTICESHIP

Nothing is known of Shayer's apprenticeship other than that he completed it and was employed as a coachpainter in Guildford by 1809. An apprenticeship to a coachpainter was usually for a period of seven years, and as an apprentice Shayer would at first have been given menial tasks such as cleaning equipment and running errands. Often apprentices were confined to these dull tasks for too long, and both John Martin and Clarkson Stanfield found it so intolerable that they ran away, although Thomas Sidney Cooper looked back on his apprenticeship with fond memory. Inevitably, an apprentice's happiness greatly depended upon the personality of his employer.

As an apprentice Shayer would have worked his way through a hierarchy of skills such as stripping, colouring and varnishing, before eventually being permitted to practise the skilled art of heraldic painting.

The process of painting a coach differed from manufactory to manufactory, and also depended upon the use to which the coach would be put. An old coach had first to be stripped and cleaned, and the dents, holes and scratches to be filled and smoothed. After being well dusted, the coach received layers of foundation coats, each coat being rubbed down lightly with powdered pumice and horsehair. The coachpainter used round and flat brushes of varying bristle designed for specific jobs such as levelling, spreading, smoothing or blending. The upper panels generally required more coats for a higher quality finish, whilst the lower panels needed to be more durable to withstand the considerable wear they received during travel. Each coach manufacturer had his own recipes for achieving the finished colours, although it was by no means unusual to use more than two dozen coats for the upper panels alone. As great emphasis was paid to the smoothness of the finish many of these coats had to be carefully rubbed down. Not until the correct finish had been achieved was the panel ready for the application of the coats of arms.

The coachpainter rarely, if ever, designed the coats of arms; his job was to reproduce accurately the meticulous design. Exactness was ensured by the method known as 'pouncing'. This entailed the use of a piece of thin paper or tracing paper (known as the pounce) upon which the outline of the design was carefully pricked through with a pin or perforating wheel. The pattern was then laid on to the panel and dusted with a bag of chalk. Small particles of dust penetrated the pin holes leaving the outline of the design on the surface to be painted. A coachpainter needed a steady hand to paint the thin and delicate flourishes of the heraldic designs, and to help him accomplish this he often used a game bird's feather in preference to a brush.

Coachpainting was an exacting trade, requiring the utmost skill, and the coachpainter took considerable pride in his work. It is not surprising to find that the practitioners of this trade were represented among the founder members of the Royal Academy, and that coachpainting formed the early training for many provincial artists in the late eighteenth and early nineteenth centuries including among others: William Allen, John Baker, Charles Catton, John Baptiste Ciprianni, Nathaniel Clarkson, Thomas Sidney Cooper, John Crome, Robert Dalton, Thomas Daniell, James Gwinn, Francis Harding, Edward Hicks, John Frederick Herring senior, John Joshua Kirby, James Lambert junior, John Martin, John Hamilton Mortimer, Alexander Nasmyth, Henry and John Ninham, James Sillett, Robert Smirke, Clarkson Stanfield, Charles Towne and Thomas Watling. Indeed, such craft apprenticeships seem to have been a most successful system for producing artists of quality. A list of artists apprenticed to portrait painters, house decorators, engravers, silversmiths, scenic artists, military draughtsmen, furniture decorators and signpainters would be considerable, and could provide food for thought to those concerned with the training of artists today.

CHICHESTER

Shayer moved from Guildford to Chichester in 1810 to work as a heraldic artist for the master coachbuilder George Parson (1764–1847). For the first year he probably lodged with his aunt, Charlotte Ayling, who lived opposite George Parson's manufactory in St. Pancras. The manufactory was a large building with a long Georgian frontage. An arch in the centre was high enough to let a carriage through to the cobbled yard behind. Each side of the arch, facing the street, were four large hinged doors opening into two showrooms in which finished carriages and coaches were displayed. In the top of the arch was a large trap door through which opening a crane hoisted and lowered carriage bodies to and from the long first floor. This consisted of the body-building loft, the trimmer's loft and the huge paintshop where Shayer worked. Round the cobbled yard behind were the wheelwright's shop, four forges, a brick-built kiln and timber stores.

William may well have met his future wife on one of her tours around the manufactory. She was George Parson's niece, Sarah Lewis Earle. Sarah's father, Robert, was the publican of the Anchor Inn, in West Street, Chichester, which still exists today, although having merged in 1910 with its old rival the adjoining Dolphin. William and Sarah were married on the 13th September 1810 at the old Subdeanery Church[1], which was then situated in the north transept of Chichester Cathedral, and afterwards took up residence directly opposite the Dolphin in one of the row of houses that then stood immediately in front of the cathedral.

Their marriage may well have been somewhat hasty for it was only seven months later on 2nd April 1811 that their first child, William Joseph Shayer, was born. On 20th April, Shayer's Aunt Charlotte decided to make a new will in which she left everything to William's sister. There was no mention of the artist and one may wonder whether the baby's early arrival had distressed her.

A year later Shayer moved to larger accommodation in Tower Street, rented from Richard Heath. Nearby, in the same street, stood the Fighting Cocks, an inn which boasted a sign allegedly painted by George Morland. It was in the same year, 1812, that the Grand Lodge of Ancients authorised the formation of the Lodge of Harmony No. 35 at Chichester, in which William Shayer was installed as Senior Warden. It was not uncommon at this time for artists to become freemasons, for they were in much demand as 'Tylers' for drawing the Lodge in chalk upon the floor, and were often initiated into the Brethren free of charge for undertaking this task. Shayer's brother-in-law, William Combes, was also a member of the Lodge. William Combes later took over the Anchor from Robert Earle, and he allowed the Lodge to use one of his rooms as a meeting place[2]. Other members of note were the fourth Duke of Richmond, Lord

[1] It was here that the artist Abraham Pether (1756–1812) married by licence Elizabeth Southon on 4th July 1780. Abraham died in 1812 at Hanover Buildings, Southampton.

[2] The Lodge met at the White Hart (once run by the parents of the marine artist C. M. Powell) until 10th June 1813. On 22nd June 1813 it moved to the Freemason's Hall in St. John's Street, remaining there until 24th October 1824 when it met in the Blücher Mercantile Room of the Anchor Inn.

John George Lennox (member of parliament for Sussex) and Thomas King (the engraver). In 1812 the Worshipful Master was Edward Atkinson Gilbert (1784–1860), the brother of Joseph Francis Gilbert (1791–1855) the landscape artist. As Senior Warden Shayer may well have become Worshipful Master at a later stage.

At this time Shayer, like most other heraldic artists, was producing work to supplement his income. He copied prints such as the portrait of the three Smith brothers[3] from a mezzotint by William Pether (see plate 4), and was commissioned by John Cooksey to devise and paint a mock coat of arms upon a truncheon, which was presented to Captain James Bryer to mark his appointment as beadle to the parish. The beadle was appointed by the vestry, and his duty was to punish petty offenders of the parish. John Cooksey, who was then wooing Captain Bryer's daughter[4], thought it would be amusing to present Bryer with a ceremonial baton with his own coat of arms, such as the Constable of Southampton held as a badge of office. Shayer, with his fine sense of humour, produced a coat of arms befitting such an occasion. Gerald Mornington, in an article in the *Hampshire Magazine* of October 1977, gives an accurate description of the heraldic design: 'It was a stroke of genius to make the outline of the central shield a reminder of that ship bisected by the Customs, its protruding keel resting on the water's edge. The shield is quartered, the first *vert* and containing three seaboots, the second *or* with three foaming tankards, the third again gold but with three churchwarden pipes, and the fourth green as the first but with three fishes. The crest has an eelspear standing upright with an oyster dredge crossed to the left, and an anchor to the right. The 'supporters' are, to the left and standing on the shore, a sailor wearing a very short blue coat over a blue and white striped jersey and white duck trousers; he holds aloft his straw hat in one hand and a bottle in the other. And on the right, her curled tail resting lightly on the waves, is a mermaid. The motto carried by a double-headed snake below, QUID RIDES, is not, as might be supposed, a vernacular reference to the Sunday afternoon trips round the harbour offered by the ferrymen, but simply Shayer's question, "At what are you laughing?"'

Shayer was also commissioned to chalk a design on the floor for a ball held by the officers of the Queen's Royal Regiment in the Assembly Rooms in North Street, Chichester, to celebrate the overthrow of Napoleon Bonaparte and the restoration of the Bourbons. The *Hampshire Telegraph* of 18th April 1814 reported 'Upwards of 200 were present, dancing was kept up with great spirit until seven the next morning. The supper was served by Mr. Andrews and the floor chalked by Mr. Shayer – both were universally admired'. The *Hampshire Chronicle* of 25th April 1814 described Shayer's work: 'The floor was chalked with superior taste, in the centre were the Queen's arms, around which were the lamb and sphynx, the insignia of the corps, with the dove and

[3] An article on the three Smiths of Chichester by Terence Mullaly appeared in the *Sussex County Magazine* Vol. 28 1954.
[4] John Cooksey married Mary Ann Bryer on 1st November 1818. In 1846 their son, Charles, married Ellen Smith. William Shayer reputedly painted a full portrait of Ellen Smith as a young girl. We have seen only a copy of this work which depicted her in a flouncy white dress and a large bonnet of the period, clutching a wooden doll. It is said that the sweep arrived as she was awaiting a sitting and seeing this delightfully pretty child, spontaneously lifted her up to kiss her and spoilt her dress.

olive branch. The whole surrounded by an elegant Egyptian border, in which were alternately introduced the rose, thistle and shamrock'.

The celebrations for the overthrow of Napoleon continued for some time, providing artists of the city the opportunity to show their talent. The *Hampshire Telegraph* of 4th July 1814 reports: 'The general illuminations at Chichester displayed the ingenuity of its artists no less than the loyalty of its inhabitants. A group of portraits representing the Prince Regent offering Peace to the Allies, through the restoration of the Bourbons painted by Shoesmith[5] gave a splendid appearance to the front of Mr. Mason's Printing Office, while two exhibitions of the Instruments of War converted into the Implements of Husbandry – the one in transparency by Shayer and the other in machinery by an ingenious young man of Biffin's manufactory – attracted the notice of the spectators. The Triumphal Arch at the entrance of the East-Gate was bestrewed with devices suitable to the auspicious occasion, and to crown the whole, the Royal and illustrious Personages passed through that city, on their return from Portsmouth, some for Petworth[6] and Brighton, and some to partake of the elegant hospitalities at Goodwood House, on the day succeeding this magnificent scene of festivity'. The most important visitors were the Prince Regent, the Tsar Alexander of Russia, Frederick William III, the King of Prussia, the Prince of Würtemburg and the Grand Duchess of Oldenburg.

At some stage Shayer's work attracted the attention of Michael Hoy (1758–1828), and it may well be that this popular and wealthy[7] merchant from Southampton visited Chichester for the celebrations. Hoy was reputed to have begun his career as an employee in a shop of a Southampton tradesman called Lomer, and was befriended by a Russian merchant who induced Hoy to come to Russia with him. The Russian treated him so handsomely that eventually he was able to return to England with an ample fortune which, by his industry, he increased until he owned extensive estates at Midanbury, Thornhill and the Isle of Wight. It was on his estate at St. Catherine's Down, Isle of Wight, that Hoy erected a 72 ft high monument, the Alexandrian Pillar, in remembrance of the visit of the Emperor of Russia to Great Britain and of his own happy and lengthy visit to Russia. He could well have acted as guide to the Tsar as he passed through Chichester, for Hoy's experience of Russia would have made him well qualified for the job. Shayer's work obviously impressed Michael Hoy for according to the *Hampshire Town and County Herald* of 13th October 1827, he 'with the munificence of a true patron of art employed Mr. Shayer until his rooms were almost covered with his works and thus gave this native artist the means and heart to prosecute his toilsome way'.

Shayer's 'way' was made more toilsome by an amusing but costly encounter with

5 Charles Shoesmith died in Southampton on 28th March 1841 'leaving a large family of orphans to bewail his loss'. A miniature of Thomas Wilmhurst by Shoesmith is reproduced in 'Changing Chichester' by M.J. Cutten and Francis Steer, Chichester Papers no. 14, page 5 plate XXI, published by Chichester City Council, 1961.

6 A painting of some of these eminent persons visiting Petworth House on 24th June 1814 by Thomas Phillips (1770–1845) is at Petworth House.

7 Some indication of his wealth is given by the expense account of his nephew, James Barlow Hoy, who inherited his estates. It is reported that in 1829 he spent £9,000 on his election campaign.

justice. In the early 1800s, it was particularly dangerous to walk on private land as gamekeepers often concealed large man traps to catch the unwary trespasser. These traps would clamp together with a force powerful enough to break a man's leg. This does not seem to have worried the artist unduly for in 1815 William Shayer and William Ayling (his uncle) were convicted and fined ten pounds and £3. 15s. 6d. respectively before Sir Charles Hamilton and Samuel Twyford for shooting on the manor and estates of W. S. Poyntz, M.P., in the parish of Cocking. A story passed down by family friends suggests that there may have been a somewhat roguish side to the artist's nature. According to their story, Shayer had invited a friend to go shooting with him, and after they spent some time at the sport William turned and said, 'I suppose you think this is my land, it's time we beat a hasty retreat!'.

Poaching, although a serious offence in the courts, was to some degree considered by the general public to be an honest man's crime. Nevertheless, by January 1816, Shayer had vacated his premises in Tower Street and, according to a freemason, had resigned from the Lodge of Harmony No. 35. Curiously, nothing is known of Shayer's life for the following three years. Furthermore, John Binstead, 'Drawing Master and respectable artist of Chichester' (with whom Shayer must have been acquainted), was hanged at Newgate in December 1815 for forging bank notes. Perhaps Shayer feared his reputation might suffer in the light of these events, and therefore considered it an appropriate time to leave Chichester. However, if this was the case, Shayer worried unnecessarily, for it is evident from the importance of the commissions that he received in 1819 (when he next appears) that he was regarded favourably.

In May of 1819 he was commissioned to paint a copy of 'The Engagement of H.M.S. *Alexander* Commanded by Sir Richard Rodney Bligh with a French Squadron under Rear-Admiral Neuilly of Three Line of Battle Shipps and One Frigate' after the painting by Thomas Guest, artist to the Duke of Clarence (see plate 7). Although the *Alexander* was captured by the French in 1794 she appears to have lost only forty killed or wounded whilst causing her opponents a loss of no fewer than four hundred and fifty men. *The Dictionary of National Biography* reports: 'In January of 1815, when the Order of the Bath was largely extended, and eighty naval officers were made K.C.B., Bligh was passed over. He felt himself aggrieved, and wrote several letters urging his claims, which were principally his sixty four years service, and his stout, although unsuccessful defence of the *Alexander*. The admiralty could not then be brought to admit that these were sufficient reason for any special reward, but five years later, under a new reign and modified ministry, he was invested with the G.C.B. He did not long enjoy the dignity, dying on the 30th April 1821'. It was possible that the copy was commissioned by Bligh to pressurise the admiralty and rally local support. Apart from this copy by Shayer, a further copy exists (by an unknown artist) and is in the reserve collection of the National Maritime Museum, Greenwich. On his death in 1821, Bligh was honoured with a funeral hatchment and it is likely that Shayer was commissioned to paint this hatchment, for his skill at heraldic painting was held in high esteem.

It is in indication of the respect in which Shayer's heraldic talents were held that he was bestowed with the honour of painting the funeral hatchment for the fourth Duke of Richmond who had died on 28th August 1819 from the bite of a fox. The fashion for funeral hatchments[8] reached its height in the Georgian era, a period when much pomp and display were usual in connection with funerals. Shayer would have been expected to produce a large diamond-shaped black-backed painting with the appropriate emblems of melancholy. The hatchment was carried in the funeral procession and was afterwards hung outside the departed one's residence where it remained for twelve months (the usual period of mourning). It was then taken down and hung in the parish church near to the memorial or place of burial of the deceased[9]. The *Brighton Herald* of 23rd October 1819 reported: 'A hatchment for our deeply lamented Lord Lieutenant of the County is painted by Shayer of Southampton (a native of Chichester) and it must be flattering to this young artist that he was selected, though at a distance on this occasion. We have before given the production of his pencil our tribute of admiration; his forte is landscape, and his style closely on that of the Smiths – we understand he is in progress with a picture for the exhibition of 1820. Powell[10] (a native of that city also) whose marine paintings are so highly esteemed, is likewise there, and is busily employed in maturing some beautiful sketches he has collected'.

In the same year Shayer painted a portrait of Prince Blücher which was hung in the Anchor Inn in what was called the Blücher Mercantile Room, the headquarters for a society known as 'the true Blues', which was probably formed to commemorate the victory at Waterloo in 1815. The painting, which has sadly been lost or destroyed, was greatly admired. The *Hampshire Telegraph* of 2nd October 1819 reported: 'The death of the veteran hero Prince Blücher is deeply lamented in Chichester where his inestimable services to his country were duly appreciated. Among other marks of respect the Blücher Mercantile Room of the Anchor Inn has his portrait on horseback painted by Shayer which is now hung with crepe and cypress and his immortal memory is drunk with profound silence and respect'. The *Brighton Herald* added that the portrait was 'esteemed a most correct likeness'.

The considerable quantity and variety of works in these years would suggest that Shayer had by 1819 (with the encouragement of Michael Hoy) made the transition from coachpainter to professional artist.

SOUTHAMPTON

In 1819 Shayer returned to Southampton, a town which at that time included among its citizens many wealthy retired officers and professional men who could be expected to provide a wider clientele.

Shayer found accommodation at 54 French Street, next door to the theatre, and he may have supplemented his income by designing or painting scenery for the theatre, for which his style would have been highly suitable. He may well have been taught scene painting by John 'Jock' Wilson, a highly respected easel and scenic artist who was

---

[8] See 'Funeral Hatchments' by Chris J. Smith in *The Amateur Historian* Vol. 2 no. 5.

[9] The fourth Duke of Richmond, Charles Lennox, was buried beneath the communion table of the cathedral of the city of Quebec. He was Governor-General and Commander-in-Chief of Canada, and he died in Upper Canada. The commission was presumably for a service in Sussex. The present whereabouts of this hatchment is unknown.

[10] Charles Martin Powell was baptised at St. Andrew's, Chichester, on 5th October 1775, and was the son of William and Jane Powell, who kept the White Hart in East Street, Chichester. Charles married Harriet Hallett by licence on 29th July 1806 at St. George's, Hanover Square, London. He died on 31st May 1824, leaving his widow and eight children 'in sad distress from his improvidence'.

described by David Roberts as being 'the Father of a race of scene painters'. The *Magazine of Art* 1884 refers to Shayer as a 'pupil of Wilson's', and it is more likely that he instructed Shayer in his capacity as scenepainter than in his position as an easel artist. Shayer was quite willing and able to turn his hand to any type of artistic activity and his skill at creating the illusion of distance with great economy of effort would have been greatly valued in the theatre. Considering the contemporary popularity of the theatre and the importance given to the scenery, it is highly improbable that Shayer would have missed the opportunity offered by the stage to exploit his artistic talents to his financial advantage. The small number of Shayer's contributions to the London exhibitions throughout his residence next to the theatre in French Street supports this supposition.

The theatre certainly had a profound influence on Shayer's style. Many of his compositions have a theatrical atmosphere, and often his figures are bathed in a low dramatic light which is quite unnatural. His lighting is for interest and effect rather than an attempt to mirror reality, and this manner is strongly reminiscent of some of the dramatically lit landscapes of Philippe Jacques de Loutherbourg, the most notable and innovative theatrical scenepainter of the eighteenth century.

Easily controlled gas lighting was first introduced to the stage in 1817, and Southampton's theatre proudly boasted its introduction in 1822, during Shayer's residence in French Street. The dramatic effect produced by this form of lighting influenced Shayer in many of his works, and he was particularly fond of concentrating the light upon the principal figures. This is carried out in a manner suggestive of actors illuminated by gas lighting, and many of his lighting and figure arrangements would translate almost directly to the stage. Shayer's use of these dramatic lighting arrangements, although admired by many, were strongly disliked by the 'followers of nature'. The *Art Journal* of 1843, for example, in reviewing his painting 'Beach Scene with Figures' remarked: 'The effect is injured by a deprivation of lights – a default observable to a certain extent in many pictures by the same hand'. Shayer's sons do not show this same strong theatrical influence.

The paintings of the seventeenth-century Dutch artists were a further influence on Shayer's stylistic development, particularly the work of Isaak and Adrian van Ostade, Nicholaes Berchem, Cornelis Dusart, Jan Wynants, Adam Pynaker and Karel Dujardin. He also learnt from the work of British artists such as George Smith of Chichester, Tobias Young, Benjamin Barker of Bath, Sir Augustus Wall Callcott, Richard Parkes Bonnington and, of course, George Morland. An old companion of Morland's, William Beardmore (1754–1827), a still-life painter, resided at Wellington Place, Southampton, so it is possible that Shayer may have seen paintings by Morland at Beardmore's studio. However, Shayer appears to have been more influenced by Morland's composition and subject matter than by his application of paint, and so his debt may have come from a close study of prints after Morland's paintings.

Shayer continued to accept the artistic odd jobs that came his way, such as the painting of inn signs, heraldic painting and the making of copies. Indeed, the *Southampton Town and County Herald* of 23rd July 1827 remarked: 'Mr. Shayer's industry and versatility of talent deserve the highest commendation', whilst the same paper had previously described the artist as a 'historical and landscape painter'. It is obvious that whilst Shayer was primarily a landscape artist he was prepared to paint anything that was required. Whenever work was lacking in Southampton he would take the opportunity to visit old friends in Chichester, where he carried out occasional work for George Parson's successor James Ewer Cutten (1783–1857). In addition to performing this wide variety of artistic tasks Shayer was able to ensure a steady income by providing instruction as a teacher of drawing in Southampton[11], and this he continued to do for a number of years.

In 1823 Shayer suffered a severe setback when, on 29th June, his wife Sarah died, leaving him alone with his five children to care for. This must have been a particularly hard time for Shayer as he was by no means established as an artist, and to earn his living and bring up his large family without the support of their mother cannot have been an easy task. It is not surprising that under such circumstances Shayer remarried within a relatively short time. In 1825 a son, Henry Thring Shayer was born, the new wife and mother being Elizabeth, daughter of William Waller, the landlord of the Duke's Head in Putney, Surrey. Elizabeth produced five children and the artist must have been hard pressed to support his new family in addition to the children of his first marriage. In a review of Shayer's work, the *Southampton Town and County Herald* of 23rd July 1827 drew attention to his plight: 'When we remember that this artist has worked his own way from obscurity to eminence, and has, by his industry, brought up most respectably a numerous family, we feel for him severe respect, and trust that for the honour of his native place, such true talent and unremitting assiduity will meet with proper patronage and due reward'. The *Hampshire Town and County Herald* of 13th October 1827 made a similar point: 'His touch is firm and free, and light, his feeling for chiaroscuro good and his distribution of lights generally happy. We fully understand how great the struggle must have been to him to rise to the height he has done with a numerous family, and his perseverance does him honour'.

Shayer possessed a lively sense of humour, which must have helped him during these difficult times. He always kept attached to his easel a small pen and ink sketch entitled 'Reform the Artist' (although always known among his family and friends as 'The Poor Artist'), which must surely have been Shayer's amusing interpretation of Morland's self portrait 'The Artist in his Studio with his Man Gibbs' which is now at the Castle Museum and Art Gallery at Nottingham. Shayer's sketch (see plate 1) depicts himself, portrayed as no more than skin and bone, and clad in rags, working at his easel. On the wall is a sign 'No Trust', which was the nineteenth-century equivalent to 'No Credit'.

Despite the impression created by 'Reform the Artist' Shayer's financial position rapidly improved, and this was no doubt helped by the opening in 1827 of the Hampshire Picture Gallery.

Henry Buchan and the Hampshire Picture Gallery

Henry Buchan is a significant figure in the history of Southampton, for not only did he do much to encourage and promote the arts, but he also helped to develop the town into an important port.

---

[11] Other notable teachers of drawing in Southampton included Tobias Young (d. December 1824) and William Beardmore (1754–1827).

Born in 1794, he began in 1814 a business in Portsmouth as a painter and decorator, presumably after successfully completing his apprenticeship in the trade. At this time house decorators were required to produce elaborate designs in elegant country mansions, demanding a high degree of accomplishment in both painting and carving, and Henry would have received expert training in both these skills.

In February 1823, he left his business at 9 Keppel Row, Portsmouth, and moved to Southampton where he opened premises at 46 High Street. Here he sold frames and, according to his advertisement, supplied artists with 'every material for drawing and painting', and continued his successful business as a house decorator for Hampshire and the surrounding counties. Through his work he would have met many artists who purchased painting materials from his shop, and many of the county's nobility and gentry, whose private collections of paintings he would have seen whilst decorating their homes. With the help of these important contacts Henry Buchan opened in 1827, at 159 High Street, Southampton, the Hampshire Picture Gallery, with an exhibition of paintings lent and paintings for sale by both modern and old masters.

According to the *Hampshire Advertiser* of 2nd August 1828, the object of the gallery was 'to gratify the public taste and curiosity at a cheap rate, and to encourage the rising merit of Artists, not only of this county, but the neighbouring counties, by giving them an opportunity of exhibiting their Works, free of expense, with the advantages of a chance of sale'. As the expense of the conveyance of paintings to and from the gallery was undertaken by Mr Buchan, the opening of the gallery must therefore have represented a considerable financial gamble. Nevertheless, the gallery appears to have been cleverly organised and it became a successful and profitable venture.

The promotion of the arts, and in particular painting, was considered of great importance throughout the nineteenth century, and consequently Henry Buchan had little difficulty finding eminent persons to help finance the gallery during the early stages. Among the dignitaries listed as patrons in the catalogue were J. Fleming, M.P., Sir W. Heathcote Bart, M.P., W. Chamberlayne, M.P., A. P. Dottin, M.P., Baring Wall, M.P., the Right Honourable Lord Lisle, Major General Gubbins and Rear Admiral Hollis. The gallery received much financial aid from members of parliament, for this exciting new venture was bound to attract considerable publicity, and by helping this worthy cause an M.P. could attract the notice and admiration of the voting public. At the same time the benefits were shared, for apart from their financial aid, the association of these eminent persons with the gallery made it a fashionable place to visit.

Henry Buchan was able to secure further finance from subscribers, who paid the fee of one guinea per annum, which entitled them to admit four of their family to the gallery. The names of the subscribers were printed in the catalogue, one of which was sent to each subscriber at the opening of every exhibition. By 9th April 1827, Henry Buchan had received nearly one hundred subscriptions, and among the subscribers[12] were J. Joliffe (the mayor of Southampton), Michael Hoy (Shayer's patron), and the artists Joseph Francis Gilbert, William Beardmore and Shayer himself. It was to the

---

[12] Other subscribers included Capt. P. N. Bligh, Commander Bullen, Mr Dashwood, Mr and Mrs Gaugain, Thomas Gray Hart, Mr Pocock, Mr N. Ogle, Mr W. Rogers and Mr J. H. Thring. A complete list appears in the *Hampshire Telegraph*, 25th June 1827.

advantage of artists to become subscribers for they were only charged five per cent on commission of sales compared with ten per cent paid by non-subscribers, and a further guinea enabled them to borrow drawings and prints for copying.

The *Southampton Herald* of 23rd July 1827 reported: 'The Gallery consists of three compartments:- an ante-room, in which, drawings, fine engravings, and a few pictures are placed; an entrance gallery, where highly finished cabinet pictures can be seen in a powerful light, and so close as to permit their high finishing to be examined; and the principal gallery. The light is good, even in the most remote parts, and it may be said that no picture is so placed that its merits cannot be fairly appreciated'. According to the *Art Journal* of May 1844 the gallery was '35 feet by 25 feet and we understand well circumstanced for light'.

The venture met with some scepticism, for many doubted the possibility of success for any gallery in Southampton, and others had wondered at Mr Buchan's unusual idea of mixing the work of provincial artists with the work of the old masters in the same exhibition. The *Southampton Herald* of 30th July 1827 found it necessary to report: 'Those who thought contemptuously, and those who spoke slightingly, of this attempt to bring our provincial painters before the public, and afford amusement and instruction to all classes, by a display of varied art, are completely put to silence by the quality of the pictures, and the general arrangements of the gallery. We sincerely trust, that now so desirable an object of attraction is founded in town, that the patronage of the inhabitants will induce the proprietor to continue his efforts'.

Although the gallery was open from seven o'clock in the morning until dusk, paintings were slow to sell. The gallery would have received much money from the entrance fee of one shilling and the sale of catalogues at sixpence each. However, sales of paintings were essential to the lasting success of the gallery, for it was successful sales that induced artists to exhibit. Fortunately the situation improved. During the first season, when three separate exhibitions were held, thirty paintings were sold, and the most popular works with the buyers proved to be by William Shayer. The gallery then settled for two exhibitions each year, one in the spring collected from provincial artists and from galleries of private gentlemen, and the other in autumn for the exhibition and sale of works by living British artists. This change of policy seems to have increased sales and reduced costs. By 1829 the sale of pictures had induced nearly double the number of artists to contribute to the gallery, some of whom had been enticed to send works from London and even further afield; such eminent artists[13] as William Collins, Thomas Barker of Bath, John Frederick Herring senior, Alexander and Patrick Nasmyth, David Roberts, James Stark, Edward William Cooke, William Daniell and members of the Williams family of painters all exhibited at Henry Buchan's gallery. The *Hampshire Telegraph* of 16th March 1829 reported: 'Henry

[13] Among the artists who exhibited at Buchan's Gallery were: A. G. Adams, E. H. Bailey, Joseph Barney junior, Benjamin Barker, Thomas James Barker, William Beardmore, Charles Bentley, William Brough, Robert William Buss, John Chase, Thomas Clater, George Cole, Richard Barrett Davis, Robert Farrier, Mrs Anne Gaugain, Philip Augustus Gaugain, Joseph Francis Gilbert, G. Glover, James Green, J. G. Grieve, Thomas Gray Hart, George T. Hastings, John Hayter, Benjamin Herring senior, James Holmes, James Inskipp, William Linton, John Neale, T. Northcote, Archer James Oliver, George Philip Reinagle, J. M. Richards and Stephen Taylor.

Buchan is returning his best thanks to the subscribers and the Public for their support in the above undertaking, and assures them that its success is beyond what he ever anticipated'.

Towards the end of his life Henry Buchan slowly retired in favour of his only son Henry Joseph Buchan, until after a long and painful illness he died on 26th October 1865, at the age of 71. Henry Buchan junior continued to promote the activities of the Hampshire Picture Gallery and was able to secure such popular attractions of the day as Barker's 'Painting of Nelson on Board the San Josef', and Rosa Bonheur's replica of 'The Horse Fair' which created a sensation as it was circulated throughout England during the 1850s, being exhibited in London, Liverpool, Manchester, Sheffield and Glasgow and attracting large crowds wherever it went.

In the year that Henry Buchan opened the Hampshire Picture Gallery, Shayer's address is given in the British Institution catalogue as 26 Grafton Street, Soho, London. This in fact was merely an accommodation address, the occupier being Leonard Wiltshire, an ornamental manufacturer, carver and gilder. Shayer remained in French Street, Southampton, until the autumn of 1828, when he moved to 158 High Street, which was rented from Henry Buchan whose gallery was next door at 159. Other artists residing in the street included William Allison at number 162, Philip Augustus Gaugain[14] (portrait painter) at number 106 and Philip Wright (marine painter) at number 86.

Shayer was visited by fellow artists, from London and further afield, whenever they were in the neighbourhood. Edward William Cooke, the marine artist, recorded in his diary on 13th July 1831: 'called on Mr. Shayer, who was glad to see me'. The following day Cooke 'went to Mr. Shayer's to breakfast at 8, he walked with me to Mr. Ogle's at Millbrook, saw him and his pictures, also his Steam Carriage. He took me over the Hants Gallery'. Cooke records that before his return journey 'Mr. Shayer sent me a basket of prawns to take home'.

The friend that Shayer and Cooke visited at Millbrook, Nathaniel Ogle, was a particularly interesting character. He invented a steam carriage, which was essentially a horseless coach driven by a large boiler situated at the back. This strange contraption was claimed to have reached speeds of up to twenty miles per hour and an average of twelve and a half miles per hour, and must have attracted the curiosity of all who encountered it.

In 1832–33 Shayer left his house in the High Street and moved to Hanover Buildings, once the home of Abraham Pether and Tobias Young, where he lived at number 10. In 1842 he was registered as living at Nursling, but this must surely have been a temporary address as within one year he had settled finally at a substantial residence in Winchester Road, Shirley, where he remained until his death thirty-six years later. According to Sir Walter Gilbey, Shayer chose to live in Shirley because of the beautiful skies that are often to be seen in that locality. Shayer named the house 'Bladon Lodge' after his wife's mother, Mary Bladon. Bladon Lodge was a large building of light yellow brick with a grey slate roof. The grounds contained stables, a coach house and a garden

[14] Philip Augustus Gaugain was Worshipful Master of 212 Royal Gloucester Lodge in 1830.

Bladon Lodge

covering three-quarters of an acre. Shayer was able to afford two servants to perform the domestic chores.

Among Shayer's closest friends, at this time, were Alderman W. H. Rogers[15], J.P. (1818–1898), who was the chief magistrate of the borough and Mayor of Southampton; and the artist Thomas Gray Hart[16] (1797–1881), who today is remembered for his watercolours in the style of J. M. W. Turner. Hart lived at Laurel Cottage, 56 Hill Lane, Shirley, and had an even larger family than Shayer's, consisting of eleven children, of whom six sons and three daughters were surviving at the time of his death in April 1881. Furthermore, Hart possessed a fine tenor voice, and was well known as a cricketer, being regarded as one of the most graceful batsmen of his day.

It is evident that Shayer was content with his existence at Shirley, for Sir Walter Gilbey in his *Animal Painters* writes 'Shayer's talent was recognized by his brother painters, some of whom, among them Sidney Cooper[17], urged him to come to London and take the place in the art world which they assured him was his. These invitations

[15] William Rogers' father was the proprietor of the Southampton Nursery and Exotic Grounds, and was appointed nurseryman and seedsman to His Majesty George IV. See *Hampshire Telegraph*, 12th February 1821.

[16] Hart's obituary in the *Hampshire Independent*, 7th May 1881, states that Shayer and Hart were warm friends.

[17] Thomas Sidney Cooper (1803–1902) expressed little praise of other artists, particularly those he may have thought to be competitors in his own subject matter, and it is unlikely that he would actively encourage such a competitor as Shayer to come to London. Perhaps Gilbey was misinformed, although it is possible that the encouraging artist was Abraham Cooper R.A. (1787–1868), a celebrated animal painter who was employed for a time at Astley's Amphitheatre, where Jock Wilson worked. J. F. Herring senior (who worked in the studio of Abraham Cooper) produced work for sale by Edward Dashwood Shayer, of which an example is in the Paul Mellon Collection.

William Shayer

Shayer resolutely declined; he was content with the life he led, could sell his works as fast as he painted them, and preferred to go his own way'.

London, however, was not to everyone's taste. A contemporary of Shayer's, the Chichester portrait painter John Lush[18], recorded in his diary: 'It has often been remarked to me by my young friends that London is the place to live in. So it is, and the place also to die in. . . . Who of a reflecting mind can but notice luxury revelling in excess? Stately mansions, princely equipages and numerous retinues and vain parade, [are] contrasted with . . . [the] abodes [of] the poor whose narrow streets and miserable abodes, filthy in the extreme and crowded to excess, breeding fevers and diseases of diverse kinds, only serve to add to their misery'.

Shayer's reluctance to leave Hampshire for London enhanced his work, for his love of the surrounding landscape is clearly evident in his paintings, but was certainly detrimental to his career. His fame would have been far more widespread had he not cut himself off from the publicity that London would have provided. Nevertheless, although Shayer never won, during his lifetime, the full measure of recognition to which his talents entitled him, his work remained extremely popular with purchasers, to such an extent that his style was often copied or imitated.

Sir Walter Gilbey writes of Shayer's paintings: 'There is no stronger proof of the demand for them than the frequency with which copies of his works are offered as

[18] See entry of September 1833: a transcript exists in the West Sussex Record Office. John Lush painted the portraits of Mr L. Binstead, Mrs Maria Combes (Shayer's sister-in-law) and one of Daniel King, the cricketer – this painting is reproduced in 'Some Inns and Alehouses of Chichester' by M. J. Cutten, Chichester Papers no. 46, published by Chichester City Council, 1964.

originals; his style is distinctive, but the expert sometimes has difficulty in distinguishing between the handiwork of Shayer and his copyists. A correspondent, formerly in the employment of a picture dealer, tells me that he was once required to submit a painting attributed to Shayer for the artist's decision. Shayer stated that the work was not his, but was one of the best copies he had ever seen.'

The nineteenth century was a period when forgery and copying of modern art works abounded. The large demand and high prices for paintings by modern artists resulted in professional copyists producing works that were then sold as originals. The high standard of craftsmanship and skill in painting prevalent throughout the century ensured that there were many persons capable of producing such forgeries. The *Art Journal* fought a vigorous campaign against such practices and in 1855 reported: 'We shall ere submit to the public a variety of anecdotes illustrative of forgeries and dealings in modern pictures; they will astonish many and disgust all. As we have said, for eight or ten years, we have laboured to expose the iniquities connected with this trade: undoubtedly there are many upright and honourable men connected with it: but there is no trade – not even horse dealing – carried on upon a system so atrocious.'

The popularity of Shayer's work (together with his retiring disposition) resulted in a remarkable number of spurious works. The collector should, therefore, be cautious, for although Shayer's paintings are a most worthwhile and satisfying way of investing money for the long term, many have been disappointed to discover their possession to be a forgery. Copyists can seldom produce works with the same enthusiasm, vision and feeling as the artist they are copying, and therefore they mostly aim to imitate an artist's worst work. This is true also of most spurious 'Shayers', which simulate his 'pot boiling' works rather than his carefully executed productions. Nevertheless they seldom reach the artist's high standards, and as with any work of art, the collector can do no better than to select paintings by virtue of quality rather than because of the name they bear, and if in doubt would be well advised to purchase from one of the reputable galleries.

Towards the end of Shayer's life his work fell out of favour with the London critics. His advanced age resulted in his producing work that really belonged to a previous generation, and although his work was quickly purchased by those willing to indulge in nostalgia, most critics found it old-fashioned and uninspiring. A critic of the *Art Journal* of 1865 was more sympathetic: 'Turning to the landscapes, we are in duty bound to give precedence to the time-honoured members who have for years adorned the gallery. Who can restrain melancholy regret that with the works of Shayer, Tennant and J. C. Ward must perish an art of which the world seems no longer worthy? The spectator while he gazes in wonder on 'The Scene in Harvest' (241) and a like scene in 'The Cornfield' (281) by Mr. Shayer, as well as other works by Mr. Tennant and Mr. Ward, cannot but feel that the present generation is not in a condition to appreciate such performances. But the time will come, we feel persuaded, when pictures like these must find their desert. Neglected they may be in modern exhibitions, they shall henceforth live for posterity'.

According to Sir Walter Gilbey, Shayer 'in his later years occasionally painted sacred subjects; in the church at Shirley there was formerly a picture of the crucifixion from his easel and presented by him'. Curiously, no records of either the presentation or the departure of this painting have been located. Indeed we are informed that during this period the church did not approve of such 'idolatry'. However, hanging in the church to this day is a particularly fine funeral hatchment in memory of Admiral Charles Bullen G.C.B. (1769–1853) who resided at Heath Cottages, Shirley. He was remembered as the last surviving officer who commanded a ship at the Battle of Trafalgar, and it was considered appropriate that he should be honoured with a funeral hatchment. The hatchment is a remarkable piece of heraldic painting, and it seems highly probable that Shayer painted it as a mark of respect for his fellow parishioner. It would be a reasonable error, when informed[19] that there was a painting by Shayer then hanging close to the altar, for Gilbey to imagine that the work was a cruxifixion.

On 9th March 1866 Shayer's second wife Elizabeth died, but the elderly artist must have been comforted by the presence of his sister-in-law, Harriet Waller, who had for many years been resident in the house. He would have needed her assistance as now he was beginning to suffer from a number of ailments, notably gout, and sometime during the early 1870s he began to go blind. He had wisely ceased painting in 1870.

In spite of his illnesses he survived his sister-in-law, who died on 6th January 1877. He was cared for by his sons Henry and Charles and by his servants, in particular his housekeeper, Miss Fanny Pusey, who was reputed to be so much part of the household that for some time she was known as Miss Shayer. William Shayer's final and fatal illness arose from the development of stones in the kidney. It is a testimony to the strength of Shayer's constitution that at this most advanced age he was able to endure the severe pains of renal colic. Eventually his kidney became so infected that he passed into a coma that lasted three days until on 21st December 1879, at the age of $92\frac{1}{2}$ years, he died[20]. He was buried in the churchyard of St. James's Church, Shirley.

The obituary in the *Southampton Times* stated: 'Mr Shayer has for some years, by the infirmities of age, [been] excluded from general society and but few are left to remember him as a social friend or companion, but those who had that advantage will sincerely bear a respectable testimony to his amiable and cheerful disposition'.

The *Hampshire Independent* of 24th December 1879 concluded: 'He had not painted for some years, consequent upon advancing age, but continued to reside in a neighbourhood very dear to him and congenial to his tastes, esteemed by a large circle of friends for his amiable disposition, and having outlived all his contemporaries he has gone down to the grave amidst the profound respect of later generations than his own.'

[19] Sir Walter Gilbey received much of his information on William Shayer from William Burrough Hill (1845–1941), an auctioneer of Southampton.

[20] William Shayer left to Henry and Charles in his will just under £1,000. The sale of his remaining works fetched at Christie's £454. 13s. 0d., whilst the remainder were bought in at £234. 14s. 2d. In considering Shayer's wealth it must be remembered that he ceased painting in 1870, so that he survived for nearly a decade on his savings, during which time he must have suffered steep medical bills.

The Use of Coachpainting Techniques

Shayer's training as a coachpainter provided him with a thorough technical grounding, and ensured that, in his eventual profession as a landscape artist, his paintings would possess a permanence that was lacking in the works of many other artists of his generation.

One skill that he acquired and used to good advantage was that of glazing, which is the art of laying transparent colours upon more opaque ones. The effect of an under-colour seen through a glazing colour is not the same as would be achieved by merely mixing the colours, for the glaze gives the colour a special quality of depth and luminosity. Although the method of glazing was used frequently during the nineteenth century by coachpainters in order to achieve the richness of colour for the panels, the technique had generally been abandoned by easel painters.

Shayer did not use glazes in the broad unifying manner of Titian but, instead, used transparent paint to enrich selected small areas. Col. Grant writes: 'His faces shaded by big rustic hats are beautiful examples of transparent painting, a fact of which Shayer was so well aware that he displayed the accomplishment almost ad nauseam. Despite his speed of production, which is inferential from the numbers of his pictures rather than the neglect in any, he puts much work into his canvas, much more than his exemplar Morland.'

Indeed, Shayer's use of transparent paint is one of the characteristic features which distinguish his work from that of his sons. Henry comes closest to using his father's techniques of transparent painting, for on tree trunks he uses the paint so thinly that in effect it becomes a glaze. However, on foregrounds and figures he does not make full use of the skill, for highlights and shadows are executed in opaque colour.

William Shayer's use of transparent paints adds considerable charm and richness to his works. In this respect, it is essential that his paintings do not suffer the harsh cleaning that is commonly applied by inadequately trained restorers, for this treatment will remove much of the thin transparent paint, to the considerable detriment of the quality and value of the painting. Whereas a skilled restorer can repair a nasty tear or hole, he can do little to remedy a harshly cleaned painting, and owners of Shayer senior's paintings are strongly advised to seek the best professional advice before embarking on any restoration.

Another skill that Shayer learnt from his work as a heraldic artist was the technique known as 'pouncing', which is a method of duplicating designs or drawings (see page 2). Shayer had to produce enough work to pay for the upkeep of his large family, and like all nineteenth-century artists without an independent income, he found it necessary to produce his share of 'pot boilers'. However, even these maintain a consistently high quality. He often painted in duplicate, saving much time by choosing and mixing colours for two paintings rather than one. Sometimes he would cunningly avoid bringing this practice to notice by, for example, altering the name of an inn sign, thus enabling two otherwise very similar paintings to be given different titles (see plates 41–42). Gradually he became more ingenious in his duplications, by such means as changing the distant scenery and varying the proportions of his canvases.

These duplications were carried out so skilfully and accurately that it is obvious that Shayer was employing some time-saving method.

At first it was considered that he may have used one of the nineteenth century's many mechanical aids to drawing, such as Wollaston's Camera Lucida. However, with the co-operation of the National Science Museum, experiments with such mechanical aids proved that while they reproduce accurately, they are so awkward and time-consuming that they are quite unsuitable as a means to speedy production of duplicate paintings.

Shayer's coachpainting method of reproducing heraldic designs on panels by the use of pouncing was quite adaptable to the reproduction of landscapes. The original drawing could be made and pricked through tracing paper, subsequently known as the 'pounce', and by laying this pounce on to canvas and dusting with chalk or graphite, the original drawing could be reproduced as many times as required. More interestingly, individual figures could be executed on separate pounces, which could then be re-arranged and used repeatedly to form new compositions.

Although there is no primary source material stating that Shayer employed such methods, the circumstantial evidence that he did so is very strong. For an artist whose output was so immense there are remarkably few surviving drawings[1]. Pounces, of course, would not survive the rigours of time, for rough handling would result in the pounce tearing along the perforations. A drawing might have been a collectable item in itself, whilst a pounce would not have been considered to be of any value or interest. More conclusively, many of Shayer's duplicate works appear in reverse. In a letter to G. S. Marshall, Shayer himself writes: 'The church and distance is correct, but the Inn in the view is the reverse way – I did not intend it to be an exact representation of any place, the subject not requiring it unless painted to commission'. It would be both impractical and impossible for an artist to copy a drawing or painting in reverse without some form of aid. He could achieve this by using a mirror, as indeed was the common practice of engravers, but this was a slow method justified only by the considerable number of engravings each plate would produce. It would be extremely time-consuming to produce part of the picture the correct way and part in reverse. However, by using a pounce it becomes a simple process of turning the pounce over and dusting through from the other side.

There is no reason why Shayer should have rejected a method of reproduction that he had often practised as a coachpainter, in favour of some other laborious method. With this in mind, it is not difficult to imagine the use to which Shayer would employ the technique. He could, for example, draw a figure on tracing paper and save time by employing one of his family to pounce the holes in the correct places. He could then arrange his composition and, as Henry and Charles's skill in painting developed, allow them to paint much of the work, with himself, as his letter suggests, 'putting the picture in good order' and 'working it up to be of the best Quality'. Using this method of production, Shayer could produce works to cover the complete price range of the art market. Works in which he contributed little catered for the lower price range, whilst those works which were solely by his own hand were placed in the higher price range.

[1] Both drawings and watercolours by William Shayer senior are remarkably rare, although there are a number of small oil studies by the artist.

It is often stated that Shayer's best period was during the 1850s, but this is not truly the case for Shayer's skill had fully developed long before that date. The reason for the misunderstanding lies in the fact that the work done by Henry and Charles was reaching maturity in these years, and consequently the works to which they contributed were from that time of a higher quality.

It would be a mistake to think that every variation of Shayer's work was produced by the pouncing method. Apart from the many spurious paintings by skilled nineteenth century copyists, many of Shayer's works were copied by his sons. It was to Shayer's advantage for his sons to reach as high a level of competence in painting as possible and he taught his sons to paint by the teaching method most favoured throughout the nineteenth century, that of making copies of paintings by the master, in this case Shayer himself.

The extent to which pouncing methods were used by artists is uncertain. According to Sidney Kitson, Cotman's method of teaching art whilst professor of drawing at King's College, London, was 'to place a drawing before each pupil, with the laconic instruction, "copy this". Then the drawing master and his assistant paced up and down the room endeavouring to keep order in a class where numbers were too large to insure adequate discipline. The boys would prick through the salient points of the design on to the paper below and draw the lines between the points'.

William Shayer's practice of reproducing his own works, and his collaborative efforts with his own sons, has encouraged the view that Shayer lacked imagination. Indeed, even Col. Grant, who has written in high praise of Shayer, writes that 'no painter would suffer more from the experience of a one-man show than he'. It seems somewhat harsh to criticise an artist for being both industrious and ingenious. One could offer the alternative view that a selective exhibition would go a long way to redressing such criticism, for setting aside the artist's own copies, as well as the copies made with his sons, and addressing our consideration only to the original versions, it becomes immediately obvious that Shayer was far more imaginative in his compositions than the majority of his contemporaries. In these paintings he produced a very great variety of original pictorial ideas and it is by these works that Shayer's status should be assessed.

Collaborative Works

As well as producing paintings with his sons in a workshop manner, William Shayer collaborated with a number of other artists, most of whom were fellow exhibitors with the Society of British Artists.

From the latter half of the eighteenth century the profession of painting in Britain was characterised by the existence of numerous families of artists. Just as the tradesman's son was expected to continue his father's profession, so too was the artist's son. This growth of families of painters in conjunction with the rising demand for landscape, marine and genre paintings created a climate ideal for a return to the co-operative workshop methods of production of an earlier age, which in turn led to a general spirit of collaboration between painters. Artists were quick to recognise the particular talents of competitors, and when these were compatible with their own talents they would arrange to collaborate for mutual advantage. Often collaboration was undertaken for reasons of friendship, as well as for commercial reasons.

Most of Shayer's joint works date from the 1850s, and as this date coincides with Edward Dashwood Shayer's emergence as an art dealer, it is likely that Edward arranged and sold many of the collaborative works. William Shayer collaborated with the following artists:

Henry Bright c. 1810–1873

Henry Bright was born at Saxmundham in Suffolk. There is some doubt as to the exact year of his birth, although it was probably 1810. He was apprenticed to a chemist in Woodbridge and was thereafter employed by Paul Squires, the Norwich chemist and soda manufacturer.

Bright spent most of his spare time painting and drawing. His achievements obviously encouraged him to attempt a career in art, and he became a pupil of Alfred Stannard (1806–1889), the younger brother of Joseph Stannard (1797–1830). Bright also received some lessons from John Berney Crome (1794–1842) and John Sell Cotman (1782–1842).

He decided to move to London where he became a most successful teacher of drawing, publishing numerous drawing books and attracting a most distinguished clientele. According to Gordon F. Roe his teaching 'is estimated to have meant as much as £2000 per annum to Bright at one portion of his career'. Among his pupils was the artist John Middleton (1828–1856) with whom he later collaborated and who, in return, influenced Bright himself.

Henry Bright, although proficient in painting figures and animals, did not execute them with the same confidence and dexterity as he did his landscapes and consequently a number of his works were produced in collaboration with other artists, among whom were Charles Baxter, J.J. Bell, Thomas Earl, John F. Herring senior, Edmund J. Niemann, Frank Stone and his son Marcus Stone. On occasions he took part in a triumvirate collaboration with Charles Baxter painting the figures, and John Frederick Herring senior the animals, within Henry Bright's landscape.

The combined skills of Shayer and Bright merge with considerable success. It appears that Henry Bright produced the landscapes leaving spacious areas for the insertion of figures and animals. It says much for the skill of Shayer that he was able to introduce figures and animals that blend with the composition and do not stand out as obvious additions by another artist. Indeed, he did this with such skill that some of their collaborative work has at times been erroneously attributed to Henry Bright alone.

Henry Bright died after a long illness on 21st September 1873 and was buried in Ipswich Cemetery.

Edward John Cobbett 1815–1899

Edward John Cobbett was born in London, where he began his career as a woodcarver. He became a pupil of Joseph William Allen (1803–1852), secretary of the Society of British Artists and drawing master of the City of London School. Cobbett became a regular exhibitor at the Society of British Artists, eventually being elected a member in 1856.

His collaboration with William Shayer was certainly not the consequence of any weakness in Cobbett's figure painting, but probably arose out of friendship and mutual admiration. Edward Cobbett's approach to figure composition seems to have had some influence on Shayer[1], whilst Shayer appears to have mildly influenced Cobbett in his choice of characters[2].

Joint works by the artists are rare. On 3rd December 1852, Henry Wallis (1804–1890), the proprietor of the French Gallery, London, sold at auction a work by the two artists entitled 'Grey Pony and Peasant Children'.

Cobbett also collaborated with the Portsmouth artist George Cole (1810–1883), the father of George Vicat Cole (1833–1893).

Thomas Creswick 1811–1869

Thomas Creswick was born in Sheffield in 1811, and later moved to Birmingham where he studied under John Vincent Barber (whose father had given lessons to David Cox). In 1828, Creswick settled in London where he exhibited at the Royal Academy, the British Institution and the Society of British Artists. He was elected a Royal Academician in 1851, and died in London in 1869. He is buried in Kensal Green Cemetery.

Creswick's figures and animals are not of the same high quality as his landscapes. He probably recognised this weakness for he worked in collaboration with many artists including Richard Ansdell, John William Bottomley, Thomas Sidney Cooper, Alfred W. Elmore, William Powell Frith, Frederick Goodall and John Phillip as well as with William Shayer.

James Godsell Middleton fl. 1826–1872

James Godsell Middleton was a genre and portrait painter, exhibiting at the Royal Academy, the British Institution and the Society of British Artists.

On 29th July 1949 Christie's sold a 'View in the New Forest' ($23\frac{1}{2}$ by $42\frac{1}{2}$ in) by William Shayer and James Godsell Middleton. It is difficult to see how James Godsell Middleton's style would have blended with Shayer's. In 1949, when the painting was catalogued by Christie's, Victorian landscape paintings in general were commanding rather low prices, and so comparatively little attention was attached to the problem of attribution. It is possible therefore that the work was not by James Godsell Middleton, but by John Middleton, the pupil of Henry Bright, whose style would have been particularly compatible with William Shayer's.

Edmund John Niemann 1813–1876

Edmund John Niemann was born in Islington in 1813, and was the son of John Diedrich Niemann, a German who had settled in England to work at Lloyd's. At the age of thirteen Edmund followed in his father's footsteps by taking employment at Lloyd's. In 1839 he left to begin a career as a painter, later becoming the secretary and

---

[1] An example of Cobbett's influence on Shayer can be seen in 'The Gleaners' at Southampton Art Gallery.

[2] An example of Shayer's influence on Cobbett can be seen in 'The Showman' at the Walker Art Gallery, Liverpool.

trustee of the Free Exhibition, as well as exhibiting at the Royal Academy, the British Institution and the Society of British Artists. His work is often confused with that of his son Edmund H. Niemann, who followed closely his father's style.

Sadly, for the two artists' styles would combine happily, collaborative works by Shayer and Niemann are extremely rare. The David Messum Gallery of Beaconsfield, Buckinghamshire, had a fine example by Niemann and Shayer which they illustrated in their advertisement published in *Country Life*, 27th December 1979. It depicted a heath with dramatically lit lime kilns in the distance and Shayer's gypsies camping in the foreground. Edmund Niemann also collaborated with Henry Bright.

Edmund died in Brixton in April 1876.

Joseph Paul Pettitt fl. 1845–1882

Joseph Paul Pettitt was a Birmingham landscape painter who exhibited at the Royal Academy, the British Institution and the Society of British Artists. Although he was a fine painter of landscapes, his figures were comparatively poor in quality. He minimised this disability in many of his works by placing the figures in the middle or far distance. In collaboration with Shayer, Pettitt painted 'Gypsies on the Road'.

Joseph Paul Pettitt died at Balsall Heath, Birmingham in 1882.

James Baker Pyne 1800–1870

James Baker Pyne was born in Bristol, where he was later apprenticed to an attorney. However, he decided to follow art as a career, supplementing his income by teaching drawing. Among his distinguished pupils were the artists William James Muller (1812–1845) and Henry Dawson (1811–1878).

Pyne moved to London in 1835, exhibiting at the Royal Academy, the British Institution and the Society of British Artists. He was elected a member of the Society of British Artists in 1841, later becoming vice-president.

His style was greatly influenced by J. M. W. Turner. However he was capable of painting works in a less 'Turneresque' style and in this more restrained manner he collaborated with Thomas Sidney Cooper, as well as with William Shayer.

John F. Tennant 1796–1872

John F. Tennant was born in Camberwell in September 1796. He began his career in a merchant's office, but soon decided that he wished to earn his living by painting. He was mostly self-taught, although he received some lessons from William Anderson.

He began by painting historical genre subjects but wisely turned his hand to coastal and landscape scenes to which his style was particularly suited. He exhibited at the Royal Academy, the British Institution and the Society of British Artists, of which he became a member in 1842.

It is said that he lived for some time in Devon and Wales, although exhibition addresses include Richmond, Hendon, Bexley, Wateringbury and Barnes.

Collaborative works by Tennant and Shayer are rare. An example, 'An Old English Homestead' was sold by Christie's on 12th May 1932. Tennant's figures can be very good, so the motive for the collaboration may have been friendship, possibly stemming from Tennant's admiration for Shayer's work; he was strongly influenced by Shayer in some of his paintings, particularly those depicting beach scenes with fisherfolk.

John Tennant died in 1872 and his obituary in the *Art Journal* testified to his agreeable disposition: 'I never heard him say unkind words to, or of, anybody.'

Alfred Vickers 1786–1868

Alfred Vickers was baptised on 10th September 1786 at St. Mary's, Newington, in Surrey. He was said to be a self-taught artist, and he exhibited at the Royal Academy, the British Institution and the Society of British Artists as well as regularly contributing to the provincial galleries. His work is often confused with that of his talented son Alfred Gomersal Vickers (1810–1837) and of A. H. Vickers.

Examples of collaborative work by William Shayer and Alfred Vickers are rare. Sotheby Belgravia illustrated a painting by the two artists in their catalogue of 9th March 1976 (lot 99), and the Polak Gallery sold another in 1980 entitled 'Wilford, Nottinghamshire'. This picture is of particular interest for, on the reverse, is a letter by Edward Shayer dated 8th May 1860 explaining that the subject depicted the birthplace of the poet Henry Kirke White (1785–1806). Edward sold the painting from his premises at 22 Pall Mall, St. James's.

The two artists' styles were not naturally compatible for Vickers' brushwork was loose and painterly, so it is likely that the two artists were friends. Indeed, in order that his figures should blend with Vickers' sketchy style, Shayer executes them in an uncharacteristically broad manner.

Dr Raymond Turley in his *Survey of Hampshire and Isle of Wight Art* writes of Vickers: 'Just as Shayer was the most prolific Hampshire exhibitor, so Alfred Vickers may claim to be the Isle of Wight artist of the nineteenth century.' As Vickers produced so many scenes of the Isle of Wight, it is likely that the artists met there whilst Shayer was visiting his daughters Emma and Anne, who were both resident on the island.

Edward Charles Williams 1807–1881

Edward Charles Williams was a member of that large family of artists whose pedigree can be traced to George Morland and James Ward. He was the eldest son of Edward Williams senior (1782–1855), and was born on 10th July 1807.

The collaboration between Edward Charles Williams and William Shayer was particularly successful, and although such works are not rare they are highly prized by collectors. Their collaborations stem from the 1850s, which suggests that they were arranged by Edward Dashwood Shayer, who probably commissioned empty landscapes to which his father skilfully added figures and animals. William Shayer also collaborated with other members of the Williams family, Sidney Richard Percy (1821–1886) and Edwin H. Boddington (born 1836). Edward Charles Williams likewise collaborated with other members of the Shayer family, namely William Joseph, Charles and Henry.

It has often been stated that William Shayer and Edward Charles Williams were related by marriage, and although it has not been possible to locate the exact connection there is some evidence to suggest that this may have been the case; on the other hand, the closest genealogical relationship may prove to be between Edward Charles Williams and William Joseph Shayer.

John H. Wilson 1774–1855

John (Jock) Wilson was born on 13th August 1774 in Ayr and was apprenticed at the age of fourteen to John Norie, a house decorator of Edinburgh. After completing his apprenticeship he received some lessons in oil painting from Alexander Nasmyth. John Wilson, like so many artists, earned his living as a teacher of drawing, which he continued to do after moving to Montrose in about 1796. Two years later he came to London where he worked as a scenepainter in various theatres, including Philip Astley's (1742–1814) Amphitheatre in the Lambeth Road.

In 1810 Wilson married a Miss Williams, and appears to have been fortunate in his choice. John Wilson's obituary in the *Art Journal* reported that he 'survived his lamented partner twenty four years, and often dwelt upon her many virtues with feelings of great emotion and tenderness'. He first exhibited at the Royal Academy in 1807, and was one of the successful competitors for premiums offered by the British Institution for a painting of 'The Battle of Trafalgar'. He sold his painting to Lord Northwick, who became one of his closest friends and a most liberal patron. Wilson became an honorary member of the Royal Scottish Academy and a founder member of the Society of British Artists, becoming president in 1827.

He was well-read, enjoying the works of Burns, Shakespeare, Pope and Scott, and was considered a brilliant conversationalist, whose fine memory and powers of recitation made him the 'centre of a delighted circle wherever he went'. During his latter years he spent much time at Briarly House, Folkestone, the residence of his son John James Wilson (1818–1875), and died there on 29th April 1855. Both John (Jock) Wilson and his son John James Wilson produced a remarkable number of works, mostly seascapes, and their styles are often confused.

No collaborative works by William Shayer and Jock Wilson have been located, although Ottley's *Dictionary of Painters and Engravers* (published in 1866 whilst Shayer was still alive) stated that Shayer was 'somewhat indebted to his co-operative study with that clever painter John (known as Jock) Wilson'. It is quite possible that Wilson painted a coastal, or even a landscape scene to which Shayer added his figures and animals. However, it is more likely that Shayer and Wilson collaborated together on some stage scenery during the 1820s. Wilson would then have been in a position to have taught Shayer various painting techniques, without necessarily being an obvious influence on his easel painting. Jock Wilson was, according to David Roberts, 'the father of a race of scenepainters including Stanfield, Tomkins, Marshall, Phillips, Pitt and Gordon, all of whom received instruction from him at various times'.

The Society of British Artists appears to have been well represented by scenic painters, and it is interesting to note that Wilson, Stanfield and Roberts were all highly influential members of the society when Shayer was elected in 1829. The relationship with Wilson may also explain Shayer's visit to Edinburgh during the 1820s.

William Shayer and the Art Unions

William Shayer obtained considerable benefit from the patronage provided by the Art Unions. These were organisations devoted to the purchase of works of art by means of a fund raised through subscription. Works of art, or the right to select them, were distributed by lot among the subscribers.

Throughout the history of patronage there have been isolated examples of works of art won by lottery, but it was not until the nineteenth century that the Art Unions emerged. They were made possible by the prosperity and growth of the middle class by means of the development of industrialisation and by the recognition of the arts as a prominent part of education.

An important precursor of the Art Unions was Monsieur M. Hennin, a distinguished amateur painter, who organised an exhibition of unsold works of art in Paris at the beginning of the nineteenth century. With the help of subscriptions and the funds raised from the exhibition, Hennin purchased a selection of works which were distributed by lot among the subscribers. Monsieur Hennin's enterprise met with such success that in 1816 he formed the 'Société des Amis des Arts'.

From France, the idea spread to Germany where Art Unions were extensively organised in most of the German states, and the Art Union of Berlin (established 1825) introduced the popular idea of distributing an engraving to each and every subscriber. The Art Union of the Rhine Provinces and Westphalia (established 1829) had high ideals, and each subscriber, in addition to receiving an engraving and the chance to win a work of art, also had the knowledge that part of his subscription went to a reserve fund for the purchase of works of art to be exhibited in public places. In the space of twenty years the Art Union of the Rhine Provinces and Westphalia commissioned twenty-four altarpieces, decorated public buildings with monumental works, and furnished the frescoes in the council-chambers at Elberfield and Aachen.

Britain sadly did not adopt the idea of a reserve fund for public works. The first Art Union of Great Britain was introduced in Scotland in 1834 and its purpose was not merely to increase patronage, but to prevent the extinction of all art other than portrait painting. According to the *Magazine of Art* (1888), before the advent of the Art Union the total expended at the Academy of Edinburgh on works of art was sometimes as little as £35 and never more than £300. The importance of the Art Unions in terms of patronage was immense. The *Magazine of Art* reported in its article that 'in 1856 it was calculated the various societies in the United Kingdom founded upon the principles already described, had expended the sum of one million sterling in promoting the interests of art'. This may have been to be an exaggeration, but nevertheless at a time when one could purchase a fine landscape for a two-figure sum the Art Unions provided a source of considerable patronage. In addition to direct financial support of the Art Unions, both interest and demand were increased by the publicity surrounding the draws and exhibitions of Art Union prizes.

The largest Art Union in Britain, and certainly the most important in William Shayer's case, was the Art Union of London, established in 1836. Each member paid a subscription fee of one guinea, entitling him to an engraving and one chance of winning a work of art in the annual draw. On the whole the engravings do not seem to have been of a very high standard, although they often received high praise from the *Art Journal*. However, in 1850, one writer in the *Art Journal* presented a more accurate account: 'One of the chief means of instruction for the public, the engravings, has signally failed in the hands of the Art Union of London; there is not one among them worth a tithe of the price any of the prints published by the Art Unions of the small German states would command'. Nevertheless the Art Union of London grew rapidly; in 1837 the sum subscribed for the advancement of art was £489 but by 1842 it had increased to £12,900.

The most important difference between the Art Union of London and earlier Art Unions was that the winners were given the freedom to select the works themselves, rather than choose from a selection purchased by a committee. Winners could select works from either the Royal Academy, the Society of British Artists, the British Institution, the Water Colour Society or the New Water Colour Society, and each winner was entitled to add his own money to the prize in order to secure a painting outside the price range of his prize.

The prizewinners showed a distinct preference for pleasant paintings that did not reflect the hardships and struggles of the age. They tended to select the contented inoffensive works provided by the many skilled landscape, marine and genre painters in which the age abounded. William Shayer's paintings were particularly suited to this popular taste, and as his figures and animals appeared so natural in characterisation, the idealised and happy landscapes in which he portrayed them appear highly convincing. Thus it is not surprising that he became one of the most popular, if not *the* most popular painter among the Art Union prizewinners.

Nevertheless, the influence of Reynold's thinking, in which art was categorised into a hierarchy according to subject matter, was still prevalent. The Art Union prizewinners were choosing 'low art' when many considered the purpose of these societies should be to encourage 'high art'. The selection procedure of the Art Union of London frequently received severe criticism, and William Shayer as a favourite with the Art Union prizewinners was the subject of one such attack in the *Art Journal* of 1847: 'To a careful examiner of this Exhibition it will be evident that there are pictures abundantly manufactured with the view to the chances of the Art Union – a state of things much to be deprecated – an alloy of evil vitiating to a great extent the real good effected by this valuable Society – to cite one striking instance of what we mean, this Exhibition presents no less than thirteen pictures by Shayer, for which the sum of five hundred and fifty-five pounds have been paid. It was never contemplated, in the institution of this Society, that any individual or individuals should produce pictures expressly for selection upon any terms by its prizeholders. If these works be examined, they will be found to be universally constructed of the same set of materials – repeated with little variation of circumstance, that variation resulting from the application of a very simple rule. This is not Art; and, difficult as the evil may seem to deal with, we are impressed with the opinion that such abuses might be obviated by some stringent regulation of the Society'.

This criticism may at first appear to be justified for William Shayer was indeed manufacturing works of art to cover the full price range of the art market but, like so many other painters, he was doing this before the emergence of the Art Unions. The Art Unions sensibly gave prizes to cover the range of the art market, so that in 1845 for example, it gave prizes of £300, £200, £150, £80, £70, £60, £50, £40, £30, £25, £15 and £10. This conveniently suited William Shayer who carried on in exactly the same fashion with the exception that he had to work harder to fulfil the increased demand for his work. The Art Union distributed his work to a wider cross-section of the public and increased his wealth, but did not encourage him to alter the type of painting he was producing. It is greatly to William Shayer's credit that at no time did he stoop to introduce the cloying sentimentality that appealed to the majority of the Victorian public.

The Influence of the Picturesque Ideal

William Shayer was of an impressionable age at a time when the vogue for the Picturesque was at its height, and as a consequence the ideal of the picturesque had a deep and lasting influence on his work.

During the eighteenth century the developing awareness of the intrinsic beauty of landscape led to tours of the British countryside becoming increasingly popular with the nobility and gentry. This was not only facilitated by improvements in roads and transport which made places like North Wales and the Lake District relatively more accessible, but was also encouraged, towards the end of the century, by the problems of travel abroad provoked by the wars on the continent. Tours of Britain rapidly took the place of the Grand Tour. One of the standard pieces of equipment carried on such tours was the Claude glass. This was a slightly convex darkened mirror, that was particularly effective for viewing sunsets as the mirror reduced the tones of the landscape producing a low-key effect reminiscent of the paintings of Claude Lorraine. By such means the tourist was encouraged to view the landscape as a painting.

This attitude was popularised through the literature of tourism, and particularly in the widely read works of the Reverend William Gilpin. Gilpin was the brother of the artist, Sawrey Gilpin, and an amateur artist himself, and so would have had some insight into the techniques and preoccupations of the landscape painter. He particularly admired the works of Salvator Rosa, Claude Lorraine, Nicolas Poussin and the Dutch landscape artists of the seventeenth century, to such an extent that in his works he constantly praised the beauty of landscape that most resembled the work of these painters. It is an indication of the popularity and importance of Gilpin's writings that the first of his series of five works, *Observations on the River Wye and several parts of South Wales . . . . relative chiefly to picturesque beauty made in the summer of the years 1770–1782*, published in 1782, had gone into five editions by 1800, when it was translated into French.

The Picturesque, already discussed as an alternative landscape gardening tradition to the smooth ideal landscape gardening of Capability Brown, was further emphasised at the turn of the century by the debate between Uvedale Price and Payne Knight (for Picturesque gardening) and Humphry Repton (who had begun to consider the re-introduction of more formal elements such as terraces, neat fences and pergolas). The Picturesque became an extremely fashionable topic for discussion, and it was by no means unknown for ladies and gentlemen to air their knowledge of it in order to impress, rather than through any genuine feeling for landscape. In Jane Austen's novel, *Sense and Sensibility*, the author indicates how worn the topic had become by the turn of the century. ' "It is very true," said Marianne, "that admiration of landscape scenery is becoming a mere jargon. Everybody pretends to feel and tries to describe with the taste and elegance of him who first defined what picturesque beauty was. I detest jargon of every kind, and sometimes I have kept my feelings to myself because I could find no language to describe them in but what was worn and hackneyed out of all sense and meaning".'

This wide use and misuse of the word 'Picturesque' led to the term becoming even more generic and vague in its meaning. This may be one reason why the importance of the Picturesque ideal in the development of British landscape art has been so greatly undervalued. To assess the importance of the Picturesque it is necessary to identify those elements that were regarded as typical of the genre. These were perceptively defined by Uvedale Price in *An Essay on the Picturesque as Compared with the Sublime and the Beautiful; and on the Use of Studying Pictures for the Purpose of Improving Real Landscape* (first edition published London 1794). Indeed Marcia Allentuck, in her essay, 'Sir Uvedale Price and the Picturesque Garden', describes him as 'the concept's most discerning, sensible, evocative and influential explicator'.

Price's aim was to elucidate the separate character of the Picturesque, and distinguish it from the Beautiful and the Sublime. The characteristics of the 'Beautiful' were considered to be, in simple terms, smoothness and gradual variation, while the 'Sublime' was defined by Edmund Burke as being characterised by 'scenes of great dimension' depicting 'awe and terror'.

The 'Picturesque' characteristically relied on those elements that were pleasing when translated into terms of paint, although not necessarily intrinsically appealing in their habitat. Large areas of flat colour, empty of incident, were of little interest and paint was regarded as visually more pleasing when it presented variety of tone and hue. The Picturesque style therefore placed great emphasis on ruggedness, variation and irregularity. Dock leaves, mosses and stones became useful additions to landscape painting as they effectively broke up the uniformity and flatness of the foreground. 'Picturesque buildings' were those that appeared most rugged, such as hovels, old cottages, run-down mills, barns, stables and ruins. In the same way, buildings overgrown or partially concealed by foliage were valued as providing further variety and interest.

'Picturesque animals' were those with rugged frames or coarse hair. In the hierarchy of animals used for the enhancement of landscapes the cow was considered to be the most picturesque followed by the donkey, old cart horse and the goat. Rotten wood, rugged fences and crockety wooden bridges were all valued as useful objects for the landscape artist adding variety and intricacy to the work. Consequently it was the dead tree, with gnarled and twisted branches, that attracted the eye of the artist of the Picturesque, particularly when it was set in juxtaposition with living trees. Uvedale Price writes: 'Near to a gnarled oak, rises the slender elegant form of a young beech, ash or birch, whose tender bark and light foliage appears more delicate when seen sideways against the rough bark and mossy head of the oak.'

The most Picturesque figures for a landscape were those that appeared rough and rugged, and so gypsies, beggars and peasants were particularly favoured. Using these aesthetic criteria, much previously ignored as ugly could be enjoyed as Picturesque. The artist of the Picturesque looked to nature for his inspiration, although he held it to be imperfect. He carefully selected and 'improved' those elements from nature that were considered to be Picturesque and composed them into an agreeable arrangement. Gilpin describes how cattle are to be arranged to the best advantage: 'Cattle are so large that when they ornament a foreground, a few are sufficient. Two cows will hardly combine. Three make a good group – either united – or when one is a little removed from the other two. If you increase the group beyond three, one or more, in proportion must necessarily be a little detached.'

It was a tendency of many painters of the Picturesque to compose their figures and animals into groups of a triangular formation. William Shayer was particularly fond of arranging his compositions in this way and, although there is no doubt that many of his groupings are quite artificially concocted, they are arranged with such care that they appear 'natural' and provide much charm in his landscapes. Shayer's foregrounds show great variety of tone and hue, and he was fond of portraying mosses, dock leaves, gnarled trees, rugged fences, cows, donkeys, goats, ragged peasants and gypsies. In a letter to Charles Combes, Shayer even uses the term: 'Yes, the old grey pony is in the picture (a prominent feature) attended by a picturesque figure talking with an old girl preparing the dinner at the fire'.

Shayer's favourite 'grey' pony, a feature of so many of his paintings, was undoubtedly Picturesque, for not only was it rugged, but it was also dappled and thus provided the necessary 'variety of tone and hue'. Compositionally it provided an area of high contrast, and in this respect he made use of his 'grey' pony in the same way that the 'white' horse was used by Philips Wouwermann.

During the early nineteenth century, as a result of the view that art was an important part of a correct and fashionable education, numerous drawing books for copying were published, and many of these were based on Picturesque principles. The most important and ambitious of these books was *Microcosm, or a Picturesque Delineation of the Arts, Agriculture, and Manufactures of Great Britain; in a Series of above a Thousand Groups of Small Figures for the Embellishment of Landscapes* by William Henry Pyne (1769–1843). *Microcosm* was published in thirty instalments of four plates, beginning in 1803. A complete second edition appeared in 1806. As a drawing master, William Shayer may well have used this popular drawing book as a teaching aid, even though the figures in Pyne's illustrations do not compare favourably with Shayer's own draughtsmanship. Shayer occasionally used some of Pyne's figures for the 'embellishment' of his own landscapes, altering and adapting them for his own convenience. He produced, for example, at least four variations of Pyne's figure of a farmer on horseback inspecting workers in a cornfield. Some of these variations appear in reverse, and on one occasion Shayer replaced the whip held by the farmer with a parasol.

Shayer's art is a fine example of the successful application of the Picturesque Ideal. The Picturesque elements that he selects are skilfully arranged and lovingly executed. The Picturesque has often been undervalued by art historians. This circumstance is partly due to the temptation, in the writing of art history, to imbue descriptive classifications with evaluative overtones. For example the word 'Romantic' is used by some almost as a term of approval. In this way a fine painting of an overgrown ruin might be described as Romantic, while a poor painting of the same subject may be dismissed with the term 'Picturesque'. It is hardly surprising therefore that the Picturesque has often been viewed in a condescending light.

Art is expressive of the full range of human emotions and experience and rightly includes the melancholy, the uplifting, the violent and the disturbing. There is room also for the pleasant and the delightful. However, because the shocking and the passionate speak with power they command more immediate attention than an art that speaks with tenderness. Vicesmimus Knox in his essay, 'On the Pleasures of a Garden' (1779), makes a point that may be considered even more pertinent today: 'Rural scenes of almost every kind are delightful to the mind of man. The verdant plain, the flowery mead, the meandering stream, the playful lamb, the warbling of birds, are all capable of exciting the gently agreeable emotions, But the misfortune is, that the greater part are hurried on in the career of life with too great rapidity to be able to give attention to that which solicits no passion.'

William Shayer and the Rural Poor

C. Reginald Grundy and F. Gordon Roe in *The Catalogue of Pictures and Drawings in the Collection of Frederick John Nettlefold* commented: 'If not unrivalled, William Shayer is, at his best, unsurpassed as a painter of the rural life of his period.' Certainly the greater part of William Shayer's work is concerned with rural life, and in this respect it will be seen that the figures in the majority of Shayer's paintings are drawn from that milieu perhaps most adequately described as 'the rural poor'.

Contemporary opinion appeared to hold the view that Shayer's works provided a truthful and accurate representation of rural and coastal life. The *Art Journal* of 1840 reported that 'his cottage scenes are true and touching'; the *Southampton Advertiser* of 31st December 1879 remarked that Shayer's paintings 'were indeed highly appreciated, being characterised by simplicity and truthfulness to nature, in which qualities lay their great charm'; the *Southampton Town and County Herald* of 23rd July 1827 described Shayer as 'a correct observer and faithful transcriber of nature', while the *Southampton Times* of 27th December 1879 described Shayer's style as 'pure and pleasing – truthful as leaves plucked from the book of Nature'.

In his book *The Dark Side of the Landscape*, Dr John Barrell warns against the uncritical acceptance of such terms of approval when used in the discussion of representations of the rural poor. Dr Barrell wisely suggests that in such cases we should ask what it was about the portrayal of the rural poor that the admiring critics wanted to believe. Viewed in this light, scenes of the rural poor during the eighteenth and early nineteenth centuries almost invariably tell us more about the art patron's view of the poor than they tell us about the poor themselves.

Shayer's paintings create an impression of rural life that is in sharp contrast with that given by William Cobbett in his *Rural Rides* (published 1830). Cobbett maintained that the living standards of the labourer were steadily declining. In writing about the valley of the Avon he comments: 'In taking my leave of this beautiful vale I have to express my deep shame, as an Englishman, at beholding the general extreme poverty of those who cause this vale to produce such quantities of food and raiment. This is, I verily believe it, the worst used labouring people upon the face of the earth. Dogs and hogs and horses are treated with more civility; and as to food and lodging, how gladly would the labourers change with them! This state of things never can continue many years! By some means or other there must be an end to it; and my firm belief is, that that end will be dreadful. In the mean while I see, and I see it with pleasure, that the common people know that they are ill used; and that they cordially, most cordially, hate those who ill-treat them.'

The poverty of labourers varied from area to area, and Cobbett spoke approvingly of both Sussex and Hampshire. Nevertheless it is obvious from Cobbett's writing that Shayer's view of the rural poor was not entirely unidealised. At the time that Shayer was painting, there existed an underlying fear, held by many wealthy British people, of the possibility of a revolution similar to that experienced in France. The rich did not wish to hang on their walls paintings of the rural poor that reminded them of this threat, nor did they wish to live with works that might prick the conscience concerning the plight of the poor. Prospective purchasers of landscape paintings looked for scenes depicting a 'deserving poor', who could be regarded as worthy of their benevolence. Indeed many of the rural labourers relied on the charity of the wealthy, for they could not survive on their wages alone. The essential characteristics of the 'deserving poor' seemed to be that they should be content with their position in life, that they should be industrious, and that they should be subservient and respectful towards the ruling classes. Furthermore, some of the rich, before providing benefaction, required the poor to demonstrate their religious piety.

It was therefore necessary, if the artist was to find purchasers for his work and avoid censure from those of influence, for him to portray the poor as 'deserving' rather than as discontented, idle or hungry, as in fact they often were. There are many paintings of the period that depict the labourer at rest, and this subject was quite acceptable to the patrons providing there was evidence in the painting to suggest that the rest was deserved, and followed a period of toil. Paintings of the period depicting peasants at rest normally include emblems of toil, such as fishstalls, wheelbarrows, toolboxes, spades or ploughs placed carefully beside the resting labourer.

It must be admitted that a minority of Shayer's scenes, usually those outside taverns, come dangerously close to depicting idlers and wasters, and we must assume these were acceptable only on account of the contented and unrebellious demeanour of the peasants. Nevertheless, Shayer's portrayal of low life did occasionally attract criticism. The *Art Journal* of March 1843, for example, remarked of his painting 'The Hampshire Farmer'[1] (see plate 19) that 'the subject naturally coarse, has been coarsely rendered'. As Shayer's painting style cannot, even by nineteenth-century taste, be described as coarse, it is clear that the characterisation of the farmer was considered to be vulgar.

Shayer's paintings of the poor are generally optimistic, and portray those happy, contented moments of life. To a great extent his work looks back nostalgically to better times, but they are executed with genuine feeling that prevents his work degenerating into mere sentimentality. Towards the end of his career, however, illness and pain undermined Shayer's characteristic optimism and his figures became increasingly despondent, their expression and stance reflecting the hardships of rural life. The weather in the landscape usually remains pleasant, but we are now aware that the

---

[1] The full title of the work was 'The Hampshire Farmer – Home Brew'd Ale'.

peasant has lived through harsh winters, rather than eternal summers (see plates 48–49).

The subject of gypsies in English art is also of considerable interest, for there was a clear disparity between the way they were represented in painting and the way they were viewed in reality. According to John Rudall, in his memoir of the Reverend James Crabb, it was popularly believed that gypsies indulged in forgery, house-breaking, highway robbery, sheep stealing, egg snatching, stealing children, poaching, horse stealing and swindling. As a class they were considered to be the lowest faction of society. Indeed Rudall writes: 'It has been the lot of Gypsies in all countries to be despised, persecuted, hated, and have the vilest things said of them.' He continues: 'The severe and unchristian-like treatment they meet with from many, only leads them to commit greater depradations. When driven by constables from their station, they retire to a more solitary place in another parish, and there remain till they are again detected, and again mercilessly driven away.' And he recounts: 'In this neighbourhood there was lately a sweeping of the common and lanes of gypsy families. Their horses and donkeys were driven off, and the sum of £3. 5s. levied on them as a fine, to pay the constables for thus afflicting them. In one tent during this distressing affair, there was found an unburied child, that had been scalded to death, its parents not having the money to defray the expense of its interment.'

It is clear from Rudall's account that Shayer's portrayal of the life of gypsies was no more unidealised than that of the poor labourer. To followers of the Picturesque Ideal gypsies were both ragged and rough, and therefore were considered highly suitable subjects for paintings. In artistic terms gypsies were looked upon as objects for the embellishment of the landscape. Uvedale Price even compares them to inanimate objects when he writes: 'In our own species objects most picturesque are to be found among the wandering tribes of gypsies and beggars, who in all the qualities that give them character, bear a close analogy to the wild forester and worn out cart horse, and again to old mills, hovels and other inanimate objects of the same kind.' Gypsies were also acceptable in art because of their 'romantic' interest, and their associations (at least in the public's mind) with the fairground, freedom and fortune telling. Indeed, the gypsy life held warm public appeal provided their encampments were not too close at hand.

Shayer's view of gypsies, although far from unidealised, was undoubtedly more advanced than that of many of his contemporaries. Gypsies were generally depicted by artists as merely 'figures in a landscape' or as exotic mystical fortune tellers, and seldom as individual personalities. Morland, who had friendly associations with the gypsies, came closest to viewing them as individuals. Shayer, however, consistently portrays them as personalities rather than objects, and even more unusually he presents them as pleasant, friendly and intelligent characters.

It is interesting to compare Shayer's attitude towards gypsy life with that of his contemporary, the Reverend James Crabb (1774–1851). Settling in Southampton in 1825, Crabb took a great interest in the welfare of the gypsies. He was mainly concerned with their spiritual welfare, and spent much time preaching to them. Nevertheless he also taught their children, helped them become apprenticed in a trade, performed marriages and distributed blankets, flannel, stockings and other necessities. Annually he would invite gypsies to his home where they would mix with dignitaries whom he invited, and be treated to a luxurious feast as well as being given clothes and other necessities.

Crabb, it is known, was much admired and respected by the gypsies. He was a close friend of Thomas Gray Hart, who was also a warm friend of Shayer's. It is therefore likely that Shayer would have been well acquainted with Crabb, and may even have accompanied him on visits to the gypsy encampments, perhaps making sketches of them whilst Crabb preached and handed out supplies.

A glance at the catalogue of Shayer's exhibited paintings soon reveals the extent to which Shayer portrayed the gypsy life, and although there is no question that the scenes he painted are idealised, they are nevertheless sympathetic. This becomes more evident when his work is seen in comparison with that of his contemporaries. To this extent, at least, Shayer is worthy of sharing with the Reverend Crabb his title, given by popular acclaim, of 'The Gypsies' Friend'.

Letters by William Shayer

The following selection of letters written by William Shayer senior are included because they convey the personality of the artist and the character of the times in which he lived.

The first letter, dated 1st May 1843, is addressed to Mr G. S. Marshall, an Art Union prizewinner, who chose for his prize William Shayer's painting 'The Village Festival'. The letter is in the Tate Gallery Files (10.3 William Shayer senior) and the painting referred to is in the reserve collection of the Tate Gallery.

The other letters are all addressed to William Shayer's favourite nephew, Charles Combes (1822–1883), son of William Combes who married Maria Earle, sister of Shayer's first wife. The letter dated 30th December 1862 and the letter dated 2nd October 1867 are in the care of the West Sussex Record Office in Chichester; the others are in private collections. The letters dated from 3rd October 1862 to 2nd January 1863 refer to two paintings, one of which is in a private collection (reproduced plate 45); the whereabouts of the other is now unknown.

Some of Shayer's writing shows signs of haste with occasional omission of conjunctions and essential punctuation. In these instances only, editorial emendations have been inserted.

Bladon Lodge
Shirley
Nr Southampton
May 1843

Sir,
I feel obliged by your selecting my picture "Village Festival" and beg to return my best thanks.

The Principal figures in the foreground are from studies made expressly for the picture, the intermediate of course imaginary. The scene is made from sketches at Alverstoke in Hampshire. The Church and distance is correct but the Inn in the view is the reverse way – I did not intend it to be an exact representation of any place, the subject not requiring it unless painted to commission.

I am Sir
Your obedient and Humble Servant
WM SHAYER

Shirley
3rd Oct 1862

Dear Charles,

Very many thanks for the handsome basket of game just to hand, it is just what we were wishing for and it comes most opportunely for an occasion[1] at the beginning of next week (not a christening) to welcome an old friend[2].

So I find all the Combes's are returned and none I trust regret 'their roaming'. My Henry[3] is on the shelf with diarrhoea and very bad, and he must have medical advice. Accounts from Harriet[4] today is similar and can't budge from the house, is an invalid in other respects and being from home is rather low spirited. The Missus[5] too is very poorly but think she will "pull through" by tomorrow.

I went yesterday to meet my Emma[6] at the station, had half an hours chat previous to her start for Edinburgh[7], she is quite well and thinks less of the journey than I do to London. She tells me my Anne[8] goes today to St. Martins[9] — believe the arrangement was made between her and Eliza[10] that it may cheer her a little previous to going to Wittering[11] as well as soothing caused by Emma's departure. The poor thing needs some change for her life is a misery[12].

Kind regards to Maria[13] and am glad you found all right and well on reaching home.

Sorry to hear your Father[14] has "sprung at heels"[15] a little, he hinted a fear of the "stiver cramp"[16] but that we know he has often had, at least so he makes out.

Mrs Shayer joins me in kind regards to all at Wittering

and remain
Dear Charles
Yrs truly
WM SHAYER

P.S. Henry returned on Tuesday was ill in London and is very ill just now – desires with Charles[17] their best remembrances.

[1] Probably the Golden Wedding anniversary of William Combes, who married Maria Earle, sister of Shayer's first wife, on 15th October 1812.
[2] Probably William Combes.
[3] Henry Thring Shayer, eldest of Shayer's sons by his second marriage.
[4] Harriet Waller, sister of Shayer's second wife.
[5] Elizabeth, Shayer's second wife.
[6] Emma Johnston, Shayer's daughter by his first marriage.
[7] Edinburgh was where Emma's husband, Dr James Townsend Oswald Johnston, studied medicine. He was born in Kirkcaldy, Fifeshire.
[8] Anne Wilkins, Shayer's daughter by his first marriage.
[9] St. Martins Street, Chichester, where William Combes lived.
[10] Eliza, daughter of William Combes and sister of Charles.
[11] Rookwood Farm, West Wittering. This was the home of Charles Combes.
[12] According to Gertrude Keller, Charles Combes' granddaughter, Anne Shayer's marriage to Dr Ernest Powell Wilkins was not a happy one. Wilkins was described as an unpleasant man who was reputed to have placed the baby on top of a wardrobe and left it there. Her impression of Anne was that she was a frightened woman, and she believes the couple eventually separated. Dr Wilkins and Anne lived at Newport, Isle of Wight.
[13] Charles Combes' wife, Maria.
[14] William Combes.
[15] A colloquial expression for 'short of money' i.e. worn through the heels of one's shoes.
[16] A stiver was originally a small coin of the Low Countries. 'Stiver cramp' was another colloquial expression for 'short of money'.
[17] Charles Waller Shayer, second of Shayer's sons by his second marriage.

Shirley
29th Nov 1862

My Dear Charles,
I have been more upset by the pair of photographs concerning Mrs Binstead's[1] likeness than you have an idea of[2]. I have called often and sent often, till I was tired, at last, by the Post this morning came the two to me (by Mrs B's consent) and expect the remainder went to Chichester at the same time. I approve of the likeness, but would have preferred the background rather lighter. I think it may be the general opinion however, we must be content, and all their apologies don't satisfy me.

Yesterday then was one of those merry days[3] at St Martins[4] which has been kept usually by juveniles. Time works wonders, and these juveniles now are of larger growth. I sincerely hope it was a very agreeable meeting. When you see your Father[5] pray repeat my desire also for his enjoying it many years to come.

I find the atmosphere have touched some of you up as well as ourselves, perhaps you have all recovered I hope so, but we here are in a sad mess. I never in my life had such a shake up, sore throat, aches in all my limbs, completely unscrewed, incapable of moving about, no sleep, in fact a regular *dimmer*. The Missus[6] and Harriet[7] perhaps worse than myself, it is so universal in this neighbourhood there is scarcely a family without the doctor in the house. We are obliged to have ours attend. He says the house[8] must be kept warm. I don't know what he would have for we have eight roaring fires going all day and have had for some time. Sausage making in consequence of this pull back is suspended, inshort, it comes under the head of forbidden food whilst these qualms predominate, and in the opinion of one or two ought to be dispensed with altogether. I can't stand that tho'.

Yes the old grey pony[9] in the picture[10] (a prominent feature) attended by a picturesque figure talking with an old gal preparing the dinner at the fire. A tent with other figures all making a good group. I feel perfectly satisfied that it will be what you will like, also I feel pleased in working it up to be of the best quality. I mean to put the other picture in good order and both shall be sent as soon as possible. I will write you previous to sending them off to you.

Kindest regards to your Maria[11] and little ones – all in West Street[12] and St Martins[13]

I remain
My Dear Charles
Yrs truly
WM SHAYER

P.S. It being Saturday the carrier has many parcels to bring out. He tells me the case with the picture is at the station but cannot bring it out till late. So as my letter is written had best send it off, the case cannot be unpacked till Monday, it will be quite safe.

Hope the photographs are arrived. I fancy myself a little better today but am not worth much now.

[1] Caroline Binstead (née Fosbrook), Charles Combes' mother-in-law.
[2] It is possible that he was using the photographs in order to portray Mrs Binstead in one of his paintings, although it is more likely that he was producing a miniature of her.
[3] This may be a reference to the birthday of William Combes, Shayer's brother-in-law, who was baptised on 17th December 1788.
[4] St. Martins Street, Chichester, where William Combes lived.
[5] William Combes.
[6] Elizabeth, Shayer's second wife.
[7] Harriet Waller, Elizabeth's sister, who was a resident in the Shayer household.
[8] Bladon Lodge.
[9] This pony was featured in many of Shayer's works and was possibly a favourite pet.
[10] This painting is illustrated plate 45.
[11] Charles Combes' wife, Maria.
[12] The family of Benjamin Binstead, Charles Combes' father-in-law. Benjamin Binstead lived at 24 West Street, Chichester. Its old coach house is now 24A West Street. The portico is reproduced in the *Victoria History of the County of Sussex* Vol. 3 page 7.
[13] The family of William Combes.

Shirley
30th December 1862

Dear Charles,
May long life, happiness and every good attend you and yours is our united wish.

I write to say the two paintings are complete and hope to get them into the frames tomorrow. Tell me the best way to direct the case that you may get it without risk or inconvenience. Say if directing it to Mr Binstead's, West Street[1] would be right, that you could on your next visit there with the car convey it yourself to Wittering[2]. I will wait your reply before I send it.

We have had quite a sick house, Mrs S[3] has been confined to her room a month with Bronchitis, is now recovering, and can move from one room to another once in the day. I trust in another week will be able to get down stairs. It has been rather serious but think now she will get over it. I have had a sharp touch of the same with gout to boot for three weeks, all right again now. A note (not a letter for it was brief enough) from your Father[4] told me he was getting on nicely, tho' not able to manage more than 4 miles a day in walking. *"I won't have it"* – it is easier to say this on paper than to do it in shoes. We shall have him joining Priory Park Cricket Club[5] next spring at this rate.

Mrs Shayer and the whole household join in kind regards to Maria[6] and all in West Street[7] and St Martins[8].

I remain
Dear Charles
Yrs truly
WM SHAYER

N.B. Let me know as soon as you can for I was tantalized with an offer for the new picture yesterday – sold another instead.

[1] Benjamin Binstead, Charles Combes' father-in-law.
[2] Rookwood Farm, West Wittering, the home of Charles Combes.
[3] Elizabeth, Shayer's second wife.
[4] William Combes, Shayer's brother-in-law.
[5] Chichester's Cricket Club, which was founded in May 1851. This was of course a joke as William Combes was then aged seventy-four. Shayer seems to have had an interest in cricket and painted a cricket match (whereabouts unknown) which was later engraved by Eugène Tily and published by Frost and Reed. Shayer was also a close friend of the artist and cricketer Thomas Gray Hart (1797–1881) who was renowned for his fine and graceful batting.
[6] Charles Combes' wife, Maria.
[7] The family of Benjamin Binstead.
[8] The family of William Combes.

Shirley
2nd January 1863

Dear Charles,

As my last told you the two pictures would be fixed in their frames on Wednesday, and are now complete, and packed in the case. So it will be best to send them off at once. Must tell you there must be great care in unpacking. On the side the direction is placed is now the top which is screwed down. Observe. Let these be drawn and with care lift it off for the new picture is fixed on the lid. All the rest will speak for itself. I think also by sending at once it will be in West Street[1] before the Gala day, then if you wish our friends to have a peep it can easily be unscrewed and readily replaced for taking it to Wittering[2]. I heartily wish you all to spend a cheerful and happy day on Monday, and as you have opportunity present my best wishes for a continuance of health, prosperity and every comfort to Mr and Mrs Binstead[3] also to all that may encircle the "jovial board".

On my telling Mrs Shayer[4] your Maria[5] hints another run to Shirley, and hopes to be prepared with material for the Veranda she smiled and hoped it would be realized, when all will be glad to receive you both, and as many as we can stow comfortably. Also if you feel a wish (as expressed in your note of a day or so) come by all means but on no account to arrange the difference for the painting, that I mean to spend in Chichester when I go there again, (which I sincerely hope to do). So pray don't think of sending it along, but piggy's appearance may be convenient to you[6].

I am pleased that Mrs S[7] is much better, and able to move from one room to another nicely, hope soon to pay off the doctor and begin with the butcher[8] by far more preferable, tho' I fear she never will be strong again, because such illness at her age is serious.

Hope your Father[9] will be one of the party on Monday. I shall think of you about four o'clock.

Mrs S and Miss Waller[10] unite with me in sincere regards to your Maria[11] and repeat the desire of seeing her (when the fine weather admits) at Shirley.

I remain
Dear Charles
Yrs very truly
Wm Shayer

P.S. Now be particular in lifting the lid of the case when you unpack, and see that all the screws are out – don't take the pictures from the case until you get to Wittering, they are screwed at the back.

Shall expect a line from you after you have examined the pictures. I think you will see an improvement in the cow picture which is in excellent order. I would have paid the carriage of the case all the way but find I cannot do so further than Portsmouth. Don't forget to write when you get the pictures home.

[1] 24 West Street, Chichester, the home of Mr and Mrs Benjamin Binstead, Charles Combes' parents-in-law.
[2] Rookwood Farm, West Wittering, the home of Charles Combes.
[3] Benjamin and Caroline Binstead. Gertrude Keller, Charles Combes' granddaughter, believed the pictures were painted for Charles and Maria Combes's Golden Wedding anniversary. However, it is more likely that the paintings were a present from Charles and Maria to Mr and Mrs Binstead on their Golden Wedding anniversary. Benjamin Binstead married Caroline Fosbrook on 5th January 1813.
[4] Elizabeth, Shayer's second wife.
[5] Charles Combes' wife, Maria.
[6] William Shayer quips that as Charles looks like a pig he should act as a piggy bank for the money that Charles owes Shayer for the paintings.
[7] Elizabeth Shayer.
[8] A reference to the family being forbidden meat by the doctor because of illness. This restriction Shayer suggests will shortly be lifted.
[9] William Combes.
[10] Harriet Waller, Elizabeth Shayer's sister.
[11] Charles Combes' wife, Maria.

Shirley
2nd October 186-

My Dear Charles,
You are a regular *"Brick"* to think of us out-of-the-world mortals. You will be pleased to know that Harriet[1] was wishing some kind friend would think of us and send along a dainty of the sort, when after about an hour two brace came from our Wittering friends much to our delight, and *I really do thank you much.* I regret that Harriet has been and still is very poorly indeed, and sometimes rather alarmingly so. We are expecting my Emma[2] shortly for a change of air, she also has been much out of sorts for some time quite an invalid and if she benefits so much good as the air of Chichester does me, fancy she will return quite restored.

I am extremely busy finishing 9 works for America[3] which must be done out of hand and glad to say are in a very forward state. They are to be packed and sent without delay to be beforehand with the November gales, causing me much anxiety and worry, else my good fellow you should have a much better and considerably longer letter than I can profitably write just now.

I sincerely hope matters concerning your brother Edward[4] are still favourable, and that he goes on improving to recovery, also that Maria's[5] eyesight will be restored to her. The thought concerning both is lamentable.

A few lines from your Father[6] the other day told me he was in tolerable good health kept up by wholesome exercise but he did not say what emolument he had for being "Marker"[7] to the sportsmen attending Wittering Manor[8].

Remember me most kindly to all in West Street[9] when next you see them and kind regards to your Maria[10].

and with much respect
Believe me to remain
Yrs sincerely
WM SHAYER

P.S. I have (as yet) no return of Gout – am thoroughly made up I trust for the winter by my late rambles in Chichester.

This letter was written on mourning paper. Presumably Shayer was mourning the loss of his wife, Elizabeth, who died on 8th March 1866. At this time the customary period of mourning for a wife was two years.

[1] Harriet Waller, sister of Shayer's now deceased second wife, Elizabeth. Harriet had been resident in the Shayer household for some years.

[2] William Shayer's daughter, Emma Johnston, who lived with her husband on the Isle of Wight.

[3] This must refer to a commission from an American dealer. The original American Art Union began in 1839 and the committee purchased works from British artists to distribute to their winners. As Shayer's work was extremely popular among the Art Union prize-winners, he would no doubt have been commissioned to produce works for the American Art Union. However, the American Art Union was short-lived and closed in 1849 when Art Unions were outlawed in the United States, so we must assume that this lead to further commissions from American dealers. In William Shayer's obituary in the *Hampshire Independent* of 24th December 1879 it was reported that 'From the time of his works becoming known in London, his name and fame were made – a Shayer continuing till today a charm for the London dealers. A goodly number of his paintings have also found their way to America'.

[4] Charles' brother, Edward Combes. Edward died shortly after this letter was written.

[5] Edward Combes' wife, Maria. Maria died the following year.

[6] William Combes, Shayer's brother-in-law.

[7] A marker marked where the game had fallen, and the task involved a considerable amount of walking. This is obviously a joke as William Combes was then seventy-nine years old. William Combes appears to have been prone to exaggeration concerning his state of health.

[8] An ironic allusion to Rookwood Farm, West Wittering, where Charles Combes lived.

[9] The Binstead family, Benjamin and Caroline Binstead being Charles Combes' parents-in-law.

[10] Charles Combes' wife, Maria.

Shirley
22 Oct 1869

My Dear Charles

We had yesterday some of our Shirley weather, dark, dull and mirky, and I had drawn my chair nearer the window to finish a little reading when I saw our Village Carrier bring in a sack whiched seemed to smile and say 'I know I am welcome'. At all events if the sack did not smile I did, and thought of your kindness. I think much of it and am greatly pleased be assured.

I regret to tell you since we last met we have had much illness in the house, the principal has fallen on Harriet[1] and she has been seriously affected, altho' much better still she is very ill and mending slowly.

Anne Wilkins[2] no doubt has detailed the sad affair, and paralysis is an awful affliction but we have good hope that the worst is over. It has added much to my depression of spirits which are seldom good at the best. My bodily health thank God is good but I have draw backs which keeps me entirely within doors, tho' I have longings for a ramble in the old quarters[3] which I fear never can be again, and my fireside ramblings about the Old City[4] must content me now and I assure you my imagination is often wandering there still.

Present my best and kindest regards to your Maria[5], Conrad[6] and Bertha[7].

I am
My Dear Charles
Yrs very truly
Wm Shayer

P.S. I am sorry my *Farm* don't produce anything worth to return in the sack.

This letter is written in larger handwriting than is usual for Shayer, which may indicate that his eyesight was deteriorating.

[1] Harriet Waller, Shayer's sister-in-law.
[2] Shayer's daughter.
[3] Chichester.
[4] Chichester.
[5] Charles Combes' wife Maria.
[6] Charles Combes' son, Conrad.
[7] Charles Combes' daughter, Emily Bertha Maria.

CHAPTER TWO

William Joseph Shayer 1811–1892

William Joseph Shayer was born in Chichester on 2nd April 1811, the eldest son of William Shayer by his first wife, Sarah Lewis Earle. As Shayer senior and his wife were living at this time directly opposite the Dolphin Hotel in one of the row of houses that once stood in front of the cathedral, it is probably here that William Joseph was born. He was baptised on 10th May 1811 at the Old Subdeanery, Chichester.

The death of William Joseph's mother, when he was only twelve, must have led to considerable hardship in the household, for at this time Shayer senior was by no means an established artist. No doubt William Joseph would have helped his father not only in the house but in the studio, grinding paints and preparing canvases while learning much from observing his father at work.

William Joseph's artistic talents were evident from an early age and, by 1828, at the age of seventeen, he was exhibiting 'Portrait of a Mare' at Henry Buchan's Hampshire Picture Gallery. The following year he exhibited a painting at the Society of British Artists as well as paintings at Buchan's Gallery, one of which was entitled 'Foxes after Landseer'. He later exhibited at the British Institution, the Royal Academy and the Royal Manchester Institution, although most of his work was sold direct to dealers and patrons.

On 23rd October 1831, at Alverstoke, William Joseph married Susannah, the daughter of Joseph Slater (b. 1762), an architect and builder of Southampton[1]. (Joseph Slater had died in 1813 and Susannah's stepfather was Daniel Brooks (1783–1854) who was later to become the first Liberal Mayor of Southampton.) Susannah gave birth on 5th May 1832 to their only child, a daughter, also named Susannah. William Joseph's occupation was listed as an animal painter and at that time the painting of animal portraits could be quite a lucrative business, for as Ben Marshall is said to have remarked: 'I discover many a man who will pay me fifty guineas for painting a horse who thinks ten guineas too much for painting his wife'. Hoping to emulate the success of other animal painters William Joseph sought his fortune closer to London and took up residence in Holborn[2]. It seems, however, that he was nevertheless unable to support his family from his paintings, for in the 1841 Census we find that he was earning his living by driving coaches. Coaching was of course in his blood, for not only did his father complete a long and arduous apprenticeship as a coachpainter but his uncle, William Combes, ran the Independent Post coach from Chichester to London. William Joseph had a high reputation in horsemanship and his skill in this field was undoubtedly an important factor in the success of his coaching paintings, for the knowledge he accumulated as a coach driver provided a rare realism and authenticity to his work. The harnessing and minor details of his coaches are depicted with a loving accuracy that would pass the scrutiny of the most critical of coaching enthusiasts.

It is interesting to note that in his book *Old Sporting*, Hugh McCausland (who was himself a skilled horseman) praises the artist for his knowledge of 'the niceties and intricacies of coaching', but of James Pollard, the most famous of coaching artists, McCausland writes 'The critical in driving lore will at times detect an error in the precise details of his coaches, and will often wish that traces, polechains and similar essentials of harnessing did not appear so consistently, simultaneously and impossibly taut'.

William Joseph's paintings tend to fall into two distinct styles. One, which can be defined as the 'documentary' style, presents horses and figures with such precision that they are obviously portraits. Hugh McCausland writes: 'Characters of the road he evidently painted from life, providing recognisable portraits of such amateur coachmen as the Duke of Beaufort, and professionals like Old George Clark of the Age, and making obvious their skill in driving as well as his own understanding of the craft.' Unfortunately the identities of many of these characters of the road are today quite unknown, but contemporaries of Shayer must have enjoyed spotting friends and rivals pictured riding the coaches in W. J. Shayer's paintings. Shayer's documentary style is characterised by restrained and careful brushwork, and is not confined to just his coaching paintings, for examples are to be found among his rural and sporting scenes.

William Joseph's alternative style could be described as 'atmospheric'. Here figures are more loosely painted, and while, in contrast to those in his documentary style, the figures could not possibly be identified, the works are compensated by the powerful sense of movement conjured by the vigour of the artist's brushwork. The figures are no longer set in stiff formal poses, but are depicted with expressive vitality. Using this style, Shayer was able to convey both a sense of movement and the atmosphere of the English weather. It was a style most suitable for racing and hunting scenes, but particularly for coaching scenes, in which William Joseph was perhaps at his best. Here

---

[1] Joseph Slater was responsible for the building of Southampton's Theatre which was opened in September 1803. It was modelled on the Theatre Royal, Drury Lane, London. The *Hampshire Telegraph and Sussex Chronicle* of 19th September 1803 reported: 'The new theatre opened here on Monday last to a crowded and brilliant audience, who testified, by the warmest applause, their admiration of the building. It is certainly in no way inferior to any theatre in the kingdom, and reflects the highest credit on the architect, Mr. Slater of this place.'

[2] A list of William Joseph's addresses is as follows:

1832   19 Carlton Place, Southampton (the previous residents being Adelaide O'Keefe and her father the dramatist John O'Keefe 1747–1833).

1834   148 High Street, Southampton (above the premises of G. B. Bishop & Co, Silk merchants).

1836   Dyers Buildings, Holborn, London.

1841   42 Princes Square, Kennington Cross (now Cleaver Square; illustrated in *London* Vol XXVI page 52)

1851   5 Kennington Green, Lambeth (now 354 Kennington Road; illustrated in *London* Vol XXVI page 46)

1855   Common, Twickenham, Middlesex

1858   5 Apsley Cottages, Twickenham

1872   Rose Villas, Belmont Road, Twickenham

1876   13 Ryder Terrace, Amyand Park, Twickenham

1890   5 St. Stephen's Villas, 77 Amyand Park Road, Twickenham

The Royal Academy Catalogue of 1885 lists his address as 191 Regent's Street. This was, in fact, the premises of the art dealer, Rudolph Ackermann junior.

he was able to convey convincingly both the pleasures and the hardships of travelling by coach. When he paints a coach travelling in the snow, he shows the passengers not perched happily on the top, but huddled in rugs with their feet buried in the straw, desperately trying to protect themselves from the bitter cold. Similarly, whereas lesser coaching artists would portray horses trotting up a steep hill with a coach behind, William Joseph's horses strain to pull the heavy loads uphill. As a true record of the coaching era, William Joseph's paintings are unsurpassed.

Generally, William Joseph's early work is painted in the documentary style whilst his later work is in the atmospheric style. However, the transition between the two styles was neither simple or smooth for commissioned portraits would often require a return to the more restrained style. Whether his paintings are of the documentary or atmospheric order, little attention is paid to the detail of the background landscapes, which are nearly always freely painted, sometimes rather clumsily so, in sharp contrast to the calm and careful character of his father's landscapes.

William Joseph's reputation as an artist has undoubtedly suffered because of his father's ability to produce works of remarkable quality. Consequently, there is an unfortunate tendency among some dealers and auction houses to attribute weak paintings in the style of Shayer senior to William Joseph Shayer. William Joseph did in fact produce some work in the style of his father, but many of the paintings of Shayer senior's imitators as well as work by Henry and Charles have found themselves wrongly attributed to William Joseph.

William Joseph occasionally collaborated with other members of the family and with the landscape artists, Charles Marshall junior (fl. 1855–1886), Charles R. Pettafor (fl. 1862–1900) and Edward Charles Williams (1807–1881). William Joseph painted the figures and animals while his collaborators painted the landscapes. Towards the end of his life he also gave kindly advice on painting to William Roebuck Read, a companion of Conrad Combes (1852–1945), whom Shayer used to visit. William Roebuck Read later wrote and illustrated a small and interesting booklet entitled *Birdham, Notes on its Village Life and Natural History*, but he was not a successful painter and his amateurish efforts provided William Joseph with much amusement.

William Joseph's work is widely known through the many prints[3] produced by C. Hunt, E. G. Hester, J. Harris, C. R. Stock, A. H. Phillips, T. Fairland, T. A. Prior, H. Papprill, J. R. Mackrell and J. H. Lynch among others. These intaglio prints were distributed by various publishers, perhaps the most notable being Rudolph Ackermann junior of 199 Regent Street. Sadly, the firm's records and correspondence were destroyed during the Second World War.

Fortunately we know much about the personality of William Joseph from family friends[4]. He was described by Gertrude Keller (1881–1968), one of his cousins, as 'a gay and frisky man full of fun, but never malicious in his humour'. A frequent expression used by him was 'Oh Lor, Oh Lor, Oh Dear, Oh Dear, Oh Lor, Oh Lor'.

At the back of his residence in Twickenham stood some livery stables with a paddock

---

[3] A list of some of these prints appears in *The Story of Sporting Prints* by Captain Frank Siltzer pp. 248–249, and many are reproduced in Frost and Reed's *Catalogue of Sporting Engravings*, 1972.
[4] These family friends were interviewed by Mervyn Cutten in 1958.

William Joseph Shayer, photo-
graphed by Walter Noah Malby in
1890.

owned by Mr William Sherley[5], M.R.C.V.S., a veterinary surgeon and horse dealer.
The stables were very popular and used by a great many citizens, but particularly by
the gentry who would turn out in their best and smartest clothes. William Joseph
would occasionally pick out the most pompous riders and discreetly shoot dried peas
at their mounts causing the horses to shill[6], to the embarrassment of the riders and to
the great amusement of the artist.

Mr Dudley Combes (1876–1964), another cousin, recounted an occasion when
William Joseph clean shaved one side of his face, leaving the other side bearded, and
appeared like this at breakfast asking his wife which side she preferred. During his
frequent trips to Keynor Farm, near Sidlesham, he enjoyed driving a miniature
carriage drawn by four goats – quite a contrast to driving a stage coach in the heyday
of the coaching era!

On 15th August 1883 his wife suffered a stroke and died. His daughter, living nearby
with her husband, must have been a considerable comfort to the artist for the latter
years of William Joseph's life were full of difficulty. Towards the end of his life he had
practically no money at all, being supported by the combined subscriptions of members
of his family such as Charles and Conrad Combes, and Frederick Keller. Every
Christmas, during these years, he spent with the Kellers at Rookwood, Chiswick Lane,
Chiswick, Middlesex; and he spent much of his summer with his cousin Charles
Combes at Rookwood Farm, West Wittering[7] or with Charles' son Conrad Combes at
Keynor Farm, Sidlesham, near Chichester. It was during his stay at Keynor Farm in
1890 that the photograph of the artist reproduced above was taken by the Chichester

[5] William Sherley's daughter, Elizabeth Jane, married W. J. Shayer's eldest grandson, Charles Williams.
[6] The word 'shill' has now fallen into a state of disuse, but meant in this context 'to make a quick sudden
movement'.
[7] A painting of this farm was executed by William Joseph Shayer in 1890.

photographer Walter Noah Malby[8] (1858–1892). Malby was renowned not only as a photographer (he won several medals including the medal of the Photographic Society of Great Britain) but also as a painter. His most famous work portrays the Goodwood Hunt, prints of which became popular in Sussex.

At Keynor Farm, weather permitting, William Joseph enjoyed long hours painting in the shade of an old damson tree, but he was gradually losing his sight and the quality of his work was declining.

William Joseph died aged 81 on 5th November 1892 at 77 Amyand Park Road, Twickenham, and was buried in the same grave as his wife and daughter and his brother Edward. There was neither a will nor letters of administration which suggests that he left no property that was considered to be of value. A tribute to the artist was made in the form of a poem printed for his funeral:

> He lived, he loved, and toiled with noble aim,
> Making life worth living for, not an idle dream.
> Nature his guide upon the road to fame,
> Reflecting around him every sunny beam
> His days flowed onward like a gurgling stream
> From springtime's budding blossoms fair and bright,
> To Summer's sunshine with its warmth and glow,
> And Autumn's sere rare tints of shade and light
> To winter wreathed in frost and drifting snow;
> Each prospect he with wondrous skill could show.
> Life-like and beautiful ever true and rare,
> Depicting nature varied and serene,
> Few have surpassed the landscape of a Shayer,
> Catching the beauties of each changing scene;
> And now amongst the noblest and the best,
> He takes his quiet everlasting rest.
>
> R.W.

---

[8] A photograph of Walter Noah Malby standing in front of his painting 'The Goodwood Hunt' appears in *Bygone Chichester* by Bernard Price.

CHAPTER THREE

Edward Dashwood Shayer 1821–1864

Regrettably little is known about William Joseph's younger brother, Edward Dashwood Shayer. He was baptised on 24th November 1821 at the parish of St. Laurence and St. John in Southampton, but before he was two years old his mother Sarah had died.

William Shayer was fond of giving the surnames of friends and relatives as middle names for his children. Edward was probably given the name of 'Dashwood' after the artist of that name who exhibited at Henry Buchan's Hampshire Picture Gallery, and who was presumably a close friend of Shayer's. In a review of an exhibition held at Buchan's Gallery the *Southampton Herald* of July 1827 reported that: 'Mr. Dashwood's picture of a calm morning on the seashore is in every respect excepting the figures equal to Mr. Shayer's'.

Edward was a witness to his sister Emma's marriage to army staff surgeon James Townsend Oswald Johnston at St. James' Church, Shirley on 17th July 1856. At this time Edward was listed in the commercial directories as a picture dealer at 22 Pall Mall, St. James', London S.W., and he obviously earned his living dealing in the works of his family as well as other artists. The address is prestigious, so we must assume it was a successful business. After 1863 he is no longer listed in the directories, and it is likely that he retired because of ill health. On 5th January 1864 Edward died from consumption at the age of forty-two. The death occurred at 177 Hanworth Road in Twickenham and he was buried on 9th January 1864 in Oak Lane Cemetery in Twickenham.

However, on Edward's death certificate his occupation is listed as 'artist', so he must also have produced a number of paintings, although as yet no signed works have been located. To judge from the standards of the other members of the family, William Shayer was an excellent teacher and Edward is likely to have reached at least a respectable standard of proficiency as a landscape painter. He would probably have collaborated with other members of the family, the most likely collaboration being with his brother, William Joseph, who lived close by in Twickenham and who is buried in the same grave.

CHAPTER FOUR
Henry Thring Shayer 1825–1894

Henry was the eldest of William Shayer senior's sons by his second marriage to Elizabeth Waller. He was baptised on 12th January 1825 in the parish of St. Laurence and St. John in Southampton. His birthplace, like that of his brother Charles, was probably in French Street, Southampton, where the Shayer family was residing in a house next door to the theatre.

Henry specialised in landscape painting, catching his father's style more closely than any other member of the family. He was at his best when painting forest glades or wooded avenues with the sunlight filtering through the trees. At times Henry reaches an excellence that makes his work extremely hard to distinguish from his father's. However, his colouring, although most pleasing, does not possess quite the subtlety that Shayer senior's work possesses, and his palette tends towards brighter and stronger colours with a preference for emerald greens. Henry's trees can be remarkably good but he is not as skilful at applying glazes as William Shayer and this is particularly noticeable in the painting of foregrounds. Often his grasses are painted with numerous little strokes in a coarse spikey fashion, without the smooth blend of textures that is characteristic of his father's work.

Henry, like his brother Charles, never married. The brothers lived and worked with their father, helping to produce paintings in a workshop environment. Under their father's direction, Henry took responsibility for much of the landscape while Charles painted the less significant figures and animals with Shayer senior adding improving touches and, especially in the more prestigious works, the most important faces, animals, figures and other features. Henry also collaborated with Charles separately, producing not only paintings in the style of their father but also sporting paintings, mainly of hunting scenes. In many of these sporting works the landscape is less carefully studied, acting only as a background to the figures and animals, some of which Henry painted. Anatomically his figures are awkward and tend to be elongated, but his animals are more competently painted, particularly his cows.

Many of Henry and Charles' collaborative works are now often exhibited and sold as William Shayer senior's and bear spurious signatures. This circumstance is detrimental not only to William Shayer's reputation but also to the standing of Henry and Charles, for although the work does not reach the very high standards of William Shayer's own work, it is nevertheless of considerable merit. Paintings by the hand of Henry alone are rare, but are of surprising quality.

Following his father's death, Henry moved with Charles to Wandsworth. Having inherited their father's wealth, the two brothers were able to live comfortably, though not luxuriously. In 1892 Henry began to go senile and on 8th December 1894, at the age of 70, he died. The death occurred at 12 Defoe Road, Tooting, the cause being record as asthenia and heart failure, and he was buried in the churchyard of St. James' Church in Shirley, Southampton. As no will was made his effects of £543. 14s. 5d. were left to his brother Charles.

CHAPTER FIVE

Charles Waller Shayer 1826–1914

Charles was the son of William Shayer's second wife, Elizabeth, and the younger brother of Henry Thring Shayer. He was baptised in the parish of St. Laurence and St. John in Southampton on 2nd August 1826, being given the name of 'Waller' after his mother's maiden name; although his name was mistakenly recorded as Charles William Shayer in the Bishop's Transcripts[1] and as Charles Walter Shayer on his death certificate.

In the 1841 census Charles is registered as residing in Putney where he went to a school situated in the High Street, run by Mr John Bird. It is not unlikely that most of the family were sent to Mr Bird for their education, and it is interesting to note that William Shayer's daughter, Anne Wilkins, named her son Robert Bird Wilkins. Although Mr Bird would have been responsible for Charles' education there is no doubt that he would have learnt the skills of painting from his father, mainly by making copies. Once Charles had reached a standard of proficiency he began to specialise in figure and animal painting. Although his work is not as distinguished in quality as his father's, at his best he is sufficiently competent to cause considerable confusion, and his work is often mistakenly attributed to Shayer senior. His figures are not as competently drawn as those of his father, particularly in the handling of elbows, shoulders and knees which often appear to be awkward and out of proportion and they are painted more coarsely and flatly, without the variation of colour and tone that is characteristic of his father's work.

Charles is at his best when painting groomed horses, and the skill with which he represents the sheen of their coats is particularly commendable. Occasionally in Charles' less carefully painted works the sheen of the horse's coats is overemphasised so that the horses appear to have been polished rather than groomed. Nevertheless Charles' horses are extremely well painted and his style naturally adapts to stable and hunting scenes.

After the death of his father Charles moved to Wandsworth with his brother Henry. He survived his brother by nearly twenty years, dying at the age of 88, on 11th February 1914. The death took place at his residence at 12 Defoe Road, Tooting[2] and he was buried in the churchyard of St. James' in Shirley in the same grave as his brother Henry. Both the tombstones of William Shayer and Henry and Charles were preserved during the alterations to St. James' Churchyard and can still be seen today.

[1] The Parish Registers of St. Laurence and St. John for this date were destroyed during the Second World War.

[2] Seffrien Alken (b. 1852), the grandson of Henry Alken (1785–1841) and son of Seffrien Alken (1821–1873), died at 44 Defoe Road, Tooting on 30th April 1913.

CHAPTER SEVEN

Abridged Pedigree

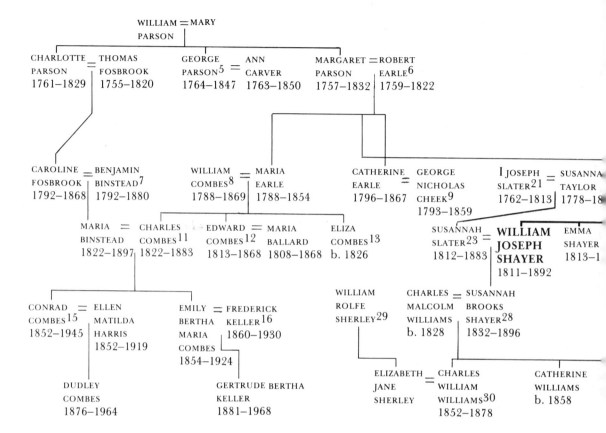

For purposes of simplification we have included only those persons of particular relevance to this study. In some cases the branches of a family are considerably longer than shown in the pedigree. Further information can be found in Brian Stewart's thesis lodged at Kent University.

[1] John Ayling, Shayer senior's grandfather, was a barber in St. Pancras, Chichester.

[2] Joseph Shayer was the landlord of the Turks Head, Spring Gardens, Southampton, and later of the Horse and Jockey (later renamed the Horse and Groom) in East Street, Southampton. He married Elizabeth Ayling by licence on 19th September 1783. Curiously there is no mention of Joseph's burial in the parish registers, the only record being a copy of the monumental inscription.

[3] Charlotte Ayling lived and died at her father's house at 7 St. Pancras, Chichester. The artist Ronald O. Dunlop R.A. (1894–1973) used these premises as his shop window, displaying his paintings there until his death.

[4] William Ayling was the landlord of the Anchor Inn, Northam, near Southampton; and later the Don Cossacks Arms, Cossack Street, Southampton. Shayer senior was caught poaching with this uncle.

[5] George Parson, coachbuilder of St. Pancras, Chichester, employed William Shayer senior as a heraldic painter. In 1807 Parson was Mayor of St. Pancras, Chichester. An apprentice of George Parson and Richard Halstead, James Stevens, was probably a natural son of the artist James Lambert junior (1741–1799); he is mentioned in Lambert's will. See *Sussex Archaeological Collections* Vol XC p. 103, 'Baldy's Garden, the Painters Lambert, and other Sussex Families' by W. H. Challen. The Lamberts' pedigree included at the end of this chapter includes the Smith brothers of Chichester.

[6] Robert Earle was landlord of the Anchor Inn, West Street, Chichester.

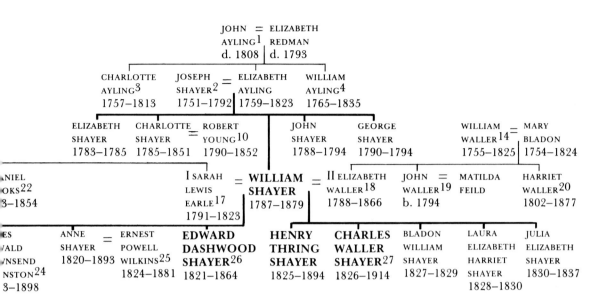

7 Benjamin Binstead was an attorney in West Street, Chichester, and a close friend of William Shayer senior. Binstead was executor to the will of Madame Amelia Idle (d. 1879) mistress of the fourth Marquess of Hertford (Charles Combes was a witness to this will). See 'Five Years Dead' by Bernard Falk 1938 pp. 34–36. Conrad Combes received a set of fish knives and forks from Madame Idle as a wedding present.

8 William Combes became landlord of the Anchor Inn, Chichester in 1814. He later farmed Rookwood Farm, West Wittering, and became a Chichester city councillor.

9 Shayer senior's brother-in-law, George Nicholas Cheek, of the Bengal Medical Establishment, served at the capture of San Sebastian and was present at Waterloo. See *The History of the Indian Medical Service* by D. G. Crawford 1914.

10 Robert Young was a slater, who later became landlord of the Crown and Anchor inn, Four Posts, Southampton. He was elected councillor for St. Mary's in 1835. Shayer senior painted a *trompe l'oeil* in black and white representing prints for Robert Young in 1814, who was then living at 21 Orchard Lane, Southampton. The *Hampshire Telegraph*, 16th February 1829, relates a serious accident to the nephew of Shayer senior: 'A most serious accident happened on Saturday to the son of Mr. R. Young of Bugle Street a fine lad about ten years of age. He was amusing himself by scattering gunpowder over a piece of lighted paper when the whole mass suddenly exploded and shattered his right hand in a most lamentable manner'.

11 Charles Combes, Shayer senior's favourite nephew, farmed Rookwood Farm in succession to his father in 1848. There is a stained glass window in memory of Charles and Maria Combes in the church of St. Peter and St. Paul, West Wittering. It is described on page 177 of *Churches and other Antiquities of West Sussex* by A. H. Peat and L. C. Halstead, published 39 East Street, Chichester, 1912.

[12] Edward Combes was landlord of the Anchor Inn, Chichester, which he took over from his father, William Combes, in 1840. Edward's wife, Maria, was a sister of William Ballard, landlord of the Dolphin Inn, next door.

[13] Eliza Combes farmed Lippering Farm, Birdham, Sussex. W. J. Shayer painted her horse, Polly.

[14] William Waller was landlord of the Dukes Head, Putney, Surrey.

[15] Conrad Combes farmed Keynor Farm, Sidlesham, and also Whitestone Farm on the Birdham Straight, where Dudley Combes was born on 31st January 1876.

[16] Frederick Keller was a shipping agent, 18 Canute Road, Southampton. He later lived in Twickenham, Middlesex; he is buried with his wife in Chichester cemetery.

[17] Sarah Lewis Earle was baptised on 25th January 1791 at the old Subdeanery church Chichester. She died on Sunday, 29th June 1823, aged 32 years (see page 9.)

[18] Elizabeth Waller married William Shayer senior between June 1823 and 12th January 1825. It has not been possible to locate the exact date of this marriage. Hilda Chaundy writes in a letter to the authors: 'Mrs Shayer was a guardian to my grandmother, Fanny Weston. As a young child my grandmother was staying as a foster child in the woods. Suddenly one day, Mrs Shayer drove up in a carriage, had all the child's clothes taken off and a set of rather grand ones put on. She was then sent to a young ladies' school run by Mrs Felix Lovell in Redbridge, near Southampton. Fanny was a shy and frightened girl and did not ask questions, but was told her parents had been drowned. Years went by and Fanny eventually married George Williams, whose business was at 13, Bedford Place, Commercial Road East, London, and they had several children. Each time there was a new birth Mrs Shayer, a tall thin nervous woman, visited her arriving in grand style by carriage. As she ended her visit she pressed a gold sovereign into the new baby's hand'.

[19] John Waller was Shayer senior's brother-in-law and executor to his will. He was a painter, plumber and estate agent of the High Street, Putney, Surrey.

[20] Harriet Waller became a resident in Shayer senior's house. She is buried in the same grave as he and his wife Elizabeth. The monumental inscription reads: 'In memory of Elizabeth, the beloved wife of William Shayer who died March 9 1866 aged 75 years. Her end was peace – Sacred to the memory of William Shayer who died December 21 1879, also of Harriet Waller'.

[21] Joseph Slater, a master builder and architect, designed the New Theatre in French Street, Southampton in 1803.

[22] Daniel Brooks, architect, surveyor and builder, became the first Liberal Mayor of Southampton in 1847–1848.

[23] Susannah Slater was baptised at St. Mary's, Southampton, on 4th October 1812. She died at 13 Ryder Terrace, Twickenham on 15th August 1883, and was buried in Oak Lane Cemetery, Twickenham, in the same grave as her husband.

[24] James Oswald Townsend Johnston M.D., Staff Surgeon to H.M. Forces, lived at Melville Street, Ryde, Isle of Wight. His wife Emma died in December 1878. They are buried in Ryde Cemetery.

[25] Ernest Powell Wilkins was a surgeon of Newport, Isle of Wight, where he established a museum in 1852. His wife, Anne, died at Newport on 13th September 1892, aged 73.

[26] Edward Dashwood Shayer was buried at Twickenham Cemetery on 9th January 1864, in the same grave as Susannah Shayer (d. 1883), W. J. Shayer (d. 1892) and Susannah Brooks Williams (d. 1869). The position of the grave was determined by no. 36 on one wall and the letters A.A. on the other.

[27] Charles Shayer is buried with his brother Henry in St. James' Churchyard, Shirley. The monumental inscription is still legible and reads: 'In memory of Henry Thring Shayer who died December 8 1894 aged 70. Also of Charles Waller Shayer brother of the above who died February 11 1914 aged 88'. The headstone has been removed from its original position and placed with others in a line on the right-hand side of the churchyard.

[28] Susannah Brooks Shayer died on 3rd April 1896 at Rookwood, Chiswick Lane, Middlesex, home of Frederick Keller.

[29] William Rolfe Sherley M.R.C.V.S., veterinary surgeon and horse dealer, resided at Twickenham. A friend of W. J. Shayer's, they often hunted together.

[30] Charles William Williams died in 1879 aged 26 and is buried in Barnes Cemetery. His widow married Lieutenant Allen Smith in 1883 at Aden.

CHAPTER SIX
Chronology

1751
William Shayer's father, Joseph, is born.

1759
William Shayer's mother, Elizabeth Ayling, is born.

1783
19th September. Joseph Shayer marries Elizabeth Ayling.

1784
5th March. Joseph Shayer takes over the occupation of the Turk's Head in Spring Gardens, Southampton.

1787
14th June. William Shayer is baptised at St. Mary's Church in Southampton.

1789
Joseph Shayer leaves the Turk's Head and moves to the Horse and Jockey in East Street, Southampton.

1792
Joseph Shayer dies.

1793
Beginning of the French Revolutionary and Napoleonic Wars.

1794
Both William Shayer's younger brothers die. George is buried on 24th January and John is buried on 7th February.

1803
Last record of the occupation of the Horse and Jockey by Elizabeth Shayer.

1809
William Shayer has completed his apprenticeship and is working as a coachpainter in Guildford.

1810
William Shayer moves to Chichester to continue his work as a coachpainter for George Parson.
13th September. William marries Sarah Lewis Earle.

1811
2nd April. William Joseph Shayer is born.

1812
William Shayer is resident in Tower Street, Chichester.
The Lodge of Harmony no. 35 is authorised by the Lodge of Ancients and William Shayer is installed as Senior Warden.

1815

February. William Shayer and William Ayling are convicted and fined for poaching.
December. John Binstead, drawing master and 'respectable artist of Chichester', is hanged at Newgate for forgery.
End of Napoleonic Wars.

1816

January. William Shayer vacates his premises in Tower Street and resigns from his Lodge.

1818

Last public execution in Chichester. Corporal Holloway is executed for the murder of Thomas Parr committed in the tap room of the Anchor. Shayer's brother-in-law, William Combes, is a witness at the trial.

1819

William Shayer is commissioned to paint the funeral hatchment for the fourth Duke of Richmond.

1820

William Shayer first exhibits at the Royal Academy.

1821

William Shayer is resident in French Street, Southampton.
23rd November. Edward Dashwood Shayer is baptised.

1823

William Shayer elected Guardian of the Poor for the parish of St. Laurence and St. John.
1st January. William Shayer's mother, Elizabeth, dies.
29th June. William Shayer's first wife, Sarah, dies.

1825

12th January. Henry Thring Shayer is baptised, William Shayer's new wife being Elizabeth Waller.

1826

2nd August. Charles Waller Shayer is baptised.

1827

June. Henry Buchan opens the Hampshire Picture Gallery. William Shayer is both a subscriber and an exhibitor.

1828

26th June. William Shayer's patron, Michael Hoy, dies. He is buried in Bayswater Cemetery, London.

1829

William Shayer is elected a member of the Society of British Artists.

1831

23rd October. William Joseph Shayer marries Susannah Slater at Alverstoke.

1834

William Shayer is resident in Hanover Buildings.

1836
The Art Union of London begins.

1839
The *Art Journal* begins. The advent of photography.

1843
William Shayer moves to Nursling, near Southampton.

1844
William Shayer moves to Bladon Lodge, Winchester Road, Shirley.

1847
George Parson, Shayer's employer, dies.

1848
Formation of the Pre-Raphaelite Brotherhood.

1850
16th October. William Shayer's daughter, Anne, marries Ernest Powell Wilkins, a surgeon of Newport, Isle of Wight.

1856
17th July. William Shayer's daughter, Emma, marries James Townsend Oswald Johnston, widower and Staff Surgeon of the Queen's Service, of Carisbrooke, Isle of Wight. Edward Dashwood Shayer is a witness.

1864
5th January. Edward Dashwood Shayer dies.

1866
9th March. William Shayer's second wife, Elizabeth, dies.

1870
William Shayer exhibits his last painting.

1877
6th January. William Shayer's sister-in-law, Harriet Waller, dies.

1879
21st December. William Shayer dies at Bladon Lodge aged $92\frac{1}{2}$ years.
Charles Shayer exhibits his only work at the Society of British Artists.

1883
15th August. William Joseph Shayer's wife, Susannah, dies.

1892
5th November. William Joseph Shayer dies aged 81.

1894
8th December. Henry Thring Shayer dies aged 70.

1914
11th February. Charles Waller Shayer dies aged 88.

CHAPTER EIGHT
Facsimile Signatures;
Facsimile Letter by William Shayer

William Shayer's training as a heraldic painter enabled him to sign his works in unusually thin paint, giving an effect similar to handwriting in ink. Although his signature often appears 'spidery' it is painted with a confidence that is extremely difficult to imitate. The thinness of his signature has, in many cases, resulted in its accidental removal during cleaning. Such works have often found themselves 're-signed', so that there are many genuine works bearing a false signature. Occasionally, mostly in early works, Shayer signed his works in the style of printed lettering. His later works, although displaying minor variations in the signature, were always signed with modest discretion in size, colour and position. Copyists on the other hand, tend to sign his name more prominently.

William Joseph Shayer uses an appropriately neat signature in his 'documentary style', while his 'atmospheric' works are signed more freely and prominently. Usually he signed his works 'W.J. Shayer', although in the hope of increasing the value the 'J' has often been removed and a spurious 'Senr' added to the end of the signature.

Edward Shayer's signature is reproduced from a parish register, and he may well have signed works in a different manner. However, Edward was not important enough during his own lifetime to merit imitation, therefore any nineteenth-century work bearing an Edward Shayer signature (which is shown to be contemporary under ultra-violet light) can safely be taken to be genuine.

Henry Shayer signs his works in a small, thin and delicate style, while Charles' signature, although similar, is usually larger and drawn in thicker paint. In many cases, again in the hope of increasing the value, the 'H' or 'C' (or 'H and C' in joint works) has been removed and replaced with a spurious 'W'.

Wm Shayer.

William Shayer senior

Wm Shayer.

William Shayer senior

Wm Shayer

William Shayer senior

W. J. Shayer

William Joseph Shayer

Edward Shayer

Edward Dashwood Shayer

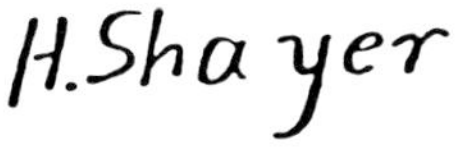

H. Shayer

Henry Thring Shayer

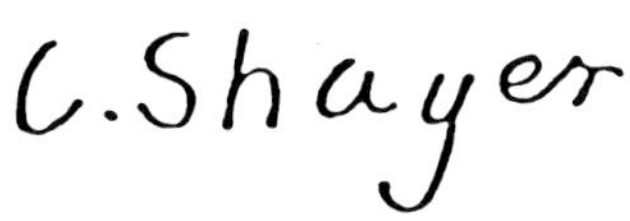

C. Shayer

Charles Waller Shayer

Shirley Oct 3
/62

Dear Charles

Very many thanks
for the handsome basket of
game just to hand, it is just
what we were wishing for
& it comes most opportunely.
for an occasion at the beginning
of next week (not a christening)
to welcome an old friend

So I find all the
Combes; are returned & none
I trust regret "their roaming"
My Henry is on the shelf
with diarrhœa & very bad, &

Facsimile letter by William Shayer senior
It is hoped that this example of William Shayer's handwriting will help identify original labels written by the
artist.

"stiver cramp" but that
we know he has often had,
at least so he makes out

     Mrs Shayer joins me in
kind regards to all at Witley
     I remain.
     Dear Charles
     Yrs truly
     Wm Shayer

W. Henry returned on Tuesday,
was ill in London & is very
ill just now – desires with
Charles their best remembrances

CHAPTER NINE
Catalogue of Exhibited Works

The following list of exhibited works, although extensive, is sadly incomplete. Sets of catalogues for the lesser provincial galleries have not always survived in their entirety, and in the case of the Hampshire Picture Gallery it has proved impossible to locate any catalogues at all. Where possible an attempt has been made to remedy this situation by referring to reviews in newspapers and periodicals. This method has not been entirely successful because after 1829 the reviews of the Hampshire Picture Gallery's exhibitions became less particularised.

Although William Shayer was in the habit of sending works unsold at the London exhibitions to one of the northern exhibitions, it was also his custom to send copies or variations of successful works. For this reason it is difficult to distinguish the exhibiting of two works under the same title from the exhibiting of the same work on two occasions. In amelioration of this problem it would be helpful to know which works were sold and to whom. However, records are far from complete and thus the fact that a work is not catalogued as sold does not necessarily mean that it was unsold.

Where possible measurements have been gleaned from exhibition catalogues and Art Union archives. These measurements were usually hastily taken during the hanging of the exhibitions and should therefore be regarded as approximations. Unfortunately today's common practice of recording height before width was not at that time always adhered to. Nevertheless in spite of these difficulties it is to be hoped that the list will be of value in the placing and dating of many works. The original spelling of the catalogues they have been corrected. The number enclosed by brackets refers to the exhibition number of the work given in the catalogue.

WILLIAM SHAYER SENIOR

1820	R.A.	(149)	Study from Nature
	R.A.	(407)	The Reaper's Repast
1823	R.A.	(170)	A Scene in the Isle of Wight, near Mirables
	R.A.	(350)	Distant View of the River Itchen, with Part of the New Forest, taken from the Grounds of J. Fleming, Esq., M.P.
			*James Fleming lived at Stoneham Park.
1824	R.A.	(150)	Children Fishing
1825	S.B.A.	(105)	Coast Scene with Figures
	S.B.A.	(106)	Boys and Donkey
	S.B.A.	(155)	Buying Fish
	S.B.A.	(298)	Coast Scene, with Fishermen

1826	S.B.A.	(2)	Fishermen
	S.B.A.	(38)	Selling Rabbits
	S.B.A.	(191)	Cattle – Evening
	S.B.A.	(277)	Pedlars
1827	B.I.	(61)	Fisherman's Cottage; 16 by 14 in
	B.I.	(235)	Landscape, Composition; 14 by 16 in
	B.I.	(306)	Forest Scene with Figures; 40 by 46 in
	B.I.	(335)	Selling Rabbits; 40 by 34 in
	H.P.G.	(–)	Fishermen Near their Boathouse
	H.P.G.	(–)	Fish Seller
	H.P.G.	(32)	Rabbit Seller; sold
	H.P.G.	(47)	Forest Scene; sold
	H.P.G.	(–)	Cattle
	H.P.G.	(–)	Donkeys
	H.P.G.	(–)	Fisherman Waiting on the Shore
	H.P.G.	(–)	Portrait of Mrs Tighes; a miniature.

*Mrs Tighes was a popular Irish poetess, and this miniature was probably a copy from her portrait engraved in the popular edition of her poem 'Psyche and Cupid' published 1811. Her portrait was engraved in the book by Caroline Watson from Comerford's miniature after a picture by Romney.

1828	B.I.	(38)	Boy and Donkies; 22 by 22 in
	B.I.	(41)	Young Crab Catchers; 23 by 22 in
	B.I.	(369)	The Fisherman's Daughter; 38 by 33 in
	B.I.	(384)	Higglers Waiting the Arrival of the Mackerel Boats, Morning; 36 by 41 in
	S.B.A.	(20)	The Gleaners
	S.B.A.	(153)	Puckester Cove, Isle of Wight
	S.B.A.	(178)	Coast Scene, Morning
	S.B.A.	(198)	Forest Scene
	S.B.A.	(218)	Coast Scene, Buying Fish
	S.B.A.	(342)	Woodman's Repast
	H.P.G.	(31)	Interior of a Cottage: Washing Day
	H.P.G.	(–)	Interior with a Horse; sold
	H.P.G.	(–)	Young Pedlars; sold
	H.P.G.	(–)	Children Anxiously Waiting Their Father's Return; sold
	H.P.G.	(–)	Study of a Cottage; sold
	H.P.G.	(–)	Buying Fish; sold
	H.P.G.	(39)	The Woodman's Repast; sold
	H.P.G.	(–)	Travellers Reposing; sold
	H.P.G.	(–)	Cattle, Evening; sold
	H.P.G.	(–)	Waiting for the Arrival of the Mackerel Boats; sold

1828	H.P.G.	(–)	Cherry Seller; sold
	H.P.G.	(–)	Fishermen's Leisure Hour; sold
	H.P.G.	(–)	Harvest Scene; sold
	H.P.G.	(–)	Smugglers; sold
1829	B.I.	(102)	Coast Scene; 20 by 18 in; bt. Turner Esq.
	B.I.	(134)	Interior of a Fisherman's Cottage; 25 by 22 in
	B.I.	(184)	Forest Scene; 21 by 19 in
	B.I.	(436)	Coast Scene; 36 by 42 in
	B.I.	(482)	A Cottager Buying Fish; 33 by 29 in
	B.I.	(487)	A Cottage Door; 25 by 22 in
	S.B.A.	(4)	Scene in the Isle of Wight
	S.B.A.	(84)	Southampton Quay – Evening
	S.B.A.	(317)	The Harvest Dinner
	H.P.G.	(–)	A Scene near Bishops Stoke
	H.P.G.	(–)	Reapers Repast
	H.P.G.	(–)	Southampton Quay
	H.P.G.	(–)	Boys Fishing at a Lock
	H.P.G.	(–)	Interior of a Stable
	H.P.G.	(–)	Scene in the New Forest
	H.P.G.	(–)	Interior of a Fisherman's Cottage
	H.P.G.	(–)	Coast Scene with Figures
	H.P.G.	(–)	Cottage Scene
1830	B.I.	(17)	Going to Market; 25 by 22 in; bt. George Cooke (father of E. W. Cooke, the marine artist)
	B.I.	(74)	Coast Scene, with Figures; 25 by 22 in
	B.I.	(75)	Scene in Hampshire; 25 by 22 in
	B.I.	(140)	Coast Scene, Squally Weather; 25 by 30 in
	B.I.	(155)	Beach Scene, Blowing Weather; 26 by 31 in
	B.I.	(159)	Scene in the New Forest; 21 by 24 in
	S.B.A.	(38)	Lane Scene – Hampshire
	S.B.A.	(235)	Scene at the Back of the Isle of Wight
	S.B.A.	(471)	Scene in the New Forest
	H.P.G.	(–)	Tivoli – after Turner; painted for Col. Henderson
	H.P.G.	(–)	Temple of Jupiter – after Turner; painted for Col. Henderson
1831	B.I.	(247)	The East Window of Netley Abbey; 25 by 22 in
	B.I.	(354)	Fisherman's Return; 26 by 22 in
	B.I.	(535)	Fishermen Mending Nets; 39 by 34 in
	S.B.A.	(43)	Coast Scene – Morning
	S.B.A.	(271)	Interior of a Cottage
	S.B.A.	(321)	Scene in Devonshire
	R.M.I.	(336)	Coast Scene – Morning
	R.M.I.	(360)	Scene in Devonshire
1832	B.I.	(271)	Scene in Wales; 37 by 51 in
	B.I.	(275)	Coast Scene – Morning; 8 by 10 in

	B.I.	(290)	Beach Scene; 10 by 11 in
	B.I.	(321)	Coast Scene with Figures; 14 by 16 in
	B.I.	(584)	Landscape with Cattle; 39 by 33 in
	S.B.A.	(58)	Scene in Wales
	S.B.A.	(60)	Coast Scene with Figures
	S.B.A.	(186)	Landscape and Cattle
	R.B.S.A.	(49)	Landscape with Cattle
1832–3	S.B.A.	(105)	Coast Scene with Figures
	S.B.A.	(233)	Beach Scene
1833	B.I.	(359)	Beach Scene; 20 by 23 in
	B.I.	(510)	Coast Scene, with Figures; 41 by 46 in
	B.I.	(517)	Scene in Sussex, Morning Effect; 38 by 45 in
	S.B.A.	(155)	Coast Scene with Figures
	S.B.A.	(207)	An Alehouse-Door
	S.B.A.	(275)	Coast Scene – Blowing Weather
	S.B.A.	(370)	Interior of a Fisherman's Cottage
	S.B.A.	(399)	Scene in Wales
1833–4	S.B.A.	(100)	Village Scene
	S.B.A.	(173)	Evening
	S.B.A.	(287)	View on the Sussex Coast
	S.B.A.	(342)	Fish Market
1834	B.I.	(46)	Scene in Wales; 49 by 45 in
	B.I.	(405)	A Boat House in Shanklin; 40 by 48 in
	B.I.	(489)	Country Inn, with Figures; 39 by 48 in
	S.B.A.	(34)	Boy and Donkey
	S.B.A.	(156)	Scene in the Isle of Wight, with Figures: Rocken End in the Distance
	S.B.A.	(253)	The Higgler
	S.B.A.	(272)	The Fresh Tap
	S.B.A.	(328)	The Harvest Field
	S.B.A.	(352)	Beach Scene, with Figures
	S.B.A.	(490)	The Tired Gleaners
	S.B.A.	(522)	Scene in Devonshire; w.c.
	R.M.I.	(139)	Rosslyn Castle; bt. E. M. Cooper Esq.
1834–5	S.B.A.	(235)	Beach Scene with Figures
	S.B.A.	(271)	The Farmer's Boy
	S.B.A.	(328)	The Parting Glass
	S.B.A.	(373)	Looking out for Mackerel Boats
1835	B.I.	(417)	Scene near Poole; 27 by 34 in
	B.I.	(441)	East Window of Netley Abbey; 39 by 42 in
	B.I.	(496)	The Prawn Fisher; 36 by 42 in
1835	B.I.	(514)	Landscape, Evening; 40 by 48 in
	S.B.A.	(20)	Village Festival

1835	S.B.A.	(76)	A Village Girl at a Spring
(*contd.*)	S.B.A.	(165)	Scene on the Sussex Coast – Morning
	S.B.A.	(244)	The Cornfield, Scene in the Isle of Wight: Hambro' Castle and Sleep Hill in the Distance
	S.B.A.	(312)	A Fish Stall
	S.B.A.	(366)	The Gipsy Fortune Teller – Scene New Forest, Hants
	S.B.A.	(402)	The Fruit Barrow
	R.M.I.	(41)	The Fruit Barrow; bt. Capt. Howard
	R.M.I.	(55)	The Gipsy Fortune Teller – Scene, New Forest Hants; bt. Capt. Howard
	R.B.S.A.	(109)	View near Poole, Dorset
	R.B.S.A.	(118)	Landscape, Composition
1836	B.I.	(389)	Gipsy Women Begging Milk; 40 by 48 in
	S.B.A.	(118)	Cottages at Clovelly, N. Devon
	S.B.A.	(143)	Water Carriers: Scene in North Devon
	S.B.A.	(281)	Waiting for the Mackerel Boats
	S.B.A.	(468)	Exterior of a Fisherman's Cottage
	R.M.I.	(99)	The Cornfield: Scene in the Isle of Wight, Hambro' Castle in the Distance
	R.M.I.	(233)	A Grazier's Cottage – Scene in Devonshire
1837	B.I.	(121)	The Poulterer; 26 by 22 in
	B.I.	(123)	Rustic Courtship; 25 by 22 in
	S.B.A.	(63)	The Cobbler
	S.B.A.	(116)	Waiting – Market Time – Morning Effect – Fog
	S.B.A.	(229)	Fisherman and Family; Scene on the Coast of Cornwall – Evening Effect
	S.B.A.	(244)	The Look-out at Clovelly, North Devon
	R.M.I.	(53)	Sea View
	R.M.I.	(163)	Ale House Door
1838	S.B.A.	(51)	Welsh Peasants
	S.B.A.	(105)	The Fisherman's Family
	S.B.A.	(175)	Scene on the Coast of Cornwall
	S.B.A.	(275)	The Expected Legacy
	S.B.A.	(300)	Scene on the Sussex Coast
	S.B.A.	(327)	The Village Inn
	R.M.I.	(35)	Coast Scene; bt. T. Cardwell Esq.
	R.B.S.A.	(111)	The Village Inn; sold
	R.B.S.A.	(146)	Scene on the Sussex Canal; sold
	R.B.S.A.	(270)	Beach Scene, Morning
1839	B.I.	(176)	Bargaining for Fish; 24 by 27 in
	B.I.	(177)	Interior of a Stable; 24 by 27 in
	B.I.	(396)	Coast Scene, Isle of Wight; 43 by 54 in
	S.B.A.	(218)	Gipsies' Camp; sold

	S.B.A.	(249)	Beach Scene, Coast of Cornwall – Morning Effect
	S.B.A.	(341)	Scene near Appledore, North Devon
	S.B.A.	(373)	Coast Scene, with Figures
	S.B.A.	(558)	Lane-scene near Christchurch, Hants; w.c.
	R.M.I.	(–)	Boy and Goat; bt. E. Buckley Esq.
	R.B.S.A.	(7)	Rustic Figures; bt. Mr Briscoe
	R.B.S.A.	(17)	Beach Scene with Figures
	R.B.S.A.	(125)	Beach Scene with Figures; sold bt. pt. A.U.P.
	R.B.S.A.	(145)	Scene near Poole Dorset, Evening; sold
	R.B.S.A.	(152)	Coast Scene
	R.B.S.A.	(191)	Interior of a Fisherman's Cottage; bt. Mr Parkes
	R.B.S.A.	(196)	Scene on the Devonshire Coast
1840	B.I.	(279)	A Prawn-fisher; 41 by 48 in
	B.I.	(296)	Devonshire Peasants; 40 by 47 in; bt. Mr Bullock Esq.
	S.B.A.	(19)	The Dairyman's Cottage
	S.B.A.	(155)	Market-people on the Beach – Morning
	S.B.A.	(200)	The Itinerant Poulterer Leaving Home
	S.B.A.	(291)	Buying Fish
	S.B.A.	(308)	Idlers
	S.B.A.	(464)	Beach-scene, with Figures
	S.B.A.	(493)	Evening
	S.B.A.	(548)	Fisherman's Children; w.c.
	R.M.I.	(82)	Beach Scene with Figures; bt. A.B. Esq.
	R.M.I.	(101)	Buying Fish; bt. A.B. Esq.
	R.M.I.	(130)	Coast Scene with Figures
	R.M.I.	(198)	Dairyman's Cottage; bt. W. Entwhistle Esq.
	R.M.I.	(253)	Cottage Scene on the Coast of Devon, Bargaining for Fish; bt. M. Schuncke
	R.M.I.	(362)	View of Southampton Old Pier, Waiting the Return of Fishing Boats
	R.M.I.	(556)	The Prawn Fisher; bt. M. Schuncke
	R.M.I.	(620)	Market People on the Beach – Morning
	R.B.S.A.	(52)	Scene on the Coast of Cornwall; bt. Howard Luckcock Esq.
	R.B.S.A.	(105)	The Itinerant Poulterer leaving home; bt. Howard Luckcock Esq.
	R.B.S.A.	(179)	The Cobbler; bt. Rev. E. Bagot
	R.B.S.A.	(185)	News of Inheritance; bt. pt. A.U.P. William Hemming Esq., Redditch
	R.B.S.A.	(321)	A Market Man; bt. Rev. E. Bagot
	R.B.S.A.	(329)	A Fisherman; bt. Rev. E. Bagot
	R.B.S.A.	(352)	Lane Scene near Niton, Isle of Wight
1840	R.B.S.A.	(360)	Harvest Time – Scene in the Isle of Wight: Hambro' castle and Ventnor in the Distance

1841	B.I.	(24)	Fisherman's Cottage, Clovelly; 40 by 47 in; bt. pt. A.U.P. A. Cox
	B.I.	(312)	Scene on the Sussex Coast, Morning; 39 by 48 in; bt. T. Miller Esq.
	S.B.A.	(77)	Outskirts of a Fair
	S.B.A.	(104)	Beacon Vale, Dorsetshire
	S.B.A.	(318)	Lane-scene, Fairfield, Isle of Wight
	S.B.A.	(354)	Loitering; bt. Mr Hollyer *features two gossiping girls
	S.B.A.	(379)	Waiting for hire; bt. Mr Wells Esq.
	S.B.A.	(466)	The Watering-place; bt. Mr Angel
	S.B.A.	(631)	The Happy Fisherman
	R.M.I.	(65)	Interior of a Stable with Figures
	R.M.I.	(72)	On the Coast of Sussex
	R.M.I.	(75)	The Happy Fisherman
	R.M.I.	(148)	Bargaining for Fish
	R.M.I.	(219)	Coast Scene with Figures
	R.M.I.	(231)	Waiting for the Ferry Boat; bt. The Association by J. Coats Esq.
	R.M.I.	(240)	On the Coast of Sussex
	R.M.I.	(459)	Lane Scene, Isle of Wight
	R.B.S.A.	(78)	Rustic Courtship
	R.B.S.A.	(127)	Sand Diggers – Scene in the New Forest, Hants – the Stone in the Distance Marks the Spot where Rufus was Slain
	R.B.S.A.	(204)	On the Sussex Coast near Hastings
	R.B.S.A.	(228)	Village Girls at a Spring; sold
	R.B.S.A.	(245)	Fishermen on the Lookout; sold
	R.B.S.A.	(358)	Tired Companions; sold
	R.B.S.A.	(371)	The Cowherd; sold
	R.B.S.A.	(388)	Contented Cottagers; sold
	L.A.	(402)	Scene on the Coast of Cornwall
	L.A.	(414)	Water Carriers; Scene in Devonshire
	L.A.	(418)	Beach Scene with Figures
1842	B.I.	(343)	A Barge Lock at Nursling, near Romsey, Hants; 42 by 53 in
	B.I.	(362)	Cattle and Figures, Autumnal Evening; 42 by 53 in; sold A.U.P.
	S.B.A.	(76)	Cattle Returning – Evening
	S.B.A.	(109)	Fisherman's Children; sold A.U.P.
	S.B.A.	(173)	The Ploughman's Dinner; sold A.U.P.
	S.B.A.	(270)	The Hard Bargain
	S.B.A.	(319)	A Diaryman's Daughter going to Market
	S.B.A.	(394)	Waiting for the Fishing-boats

William Shayer: 'At the Bell Inn, Cadnam, New Forest'; signed; 40 by 50 in; photograph by courtesy of Richard Green Galleries, London.

William Shayer: 'Outside the Fisherman's Cottage'; signed and dated 1836; 28 by 36 in; photograph by courtesy of Richard Green Galleries, London.

William Shayer: 'The Milk Maid'; signed; 34 by 44 in; photograph by courtesy of Richard Green Galleries, London.

	S.B.A.	(468)	Scene on the Sussex Coast, near Hastings
	S.B.A.	(636)	Interior of a Stable; 20 by 30 in; A.U.P. bt. S. Solly Esq.; engraved
	R.M.I.	(53)	Beach Scene Isle of Wight – Evening
	R.M.I.	(62)	Interior of a Fisherman's Cottage
	R.M.I.	(72)	Scene on the coast of Cornwall
	R.M.I.	(158)	Coming through the Lock
	R.M.I.	(164)	The Fisherman's Daughter
	R.M.I.	(298)	Waiting for the Ferry
	R.M.I.	(362)	The Hard Bargain
	R.B.S.A.	(82)	The Cow-herd, Scene on Badesley Heath
	R.B.S.A.	(96)	Coast Scene – Fisherman Mending his Nets
	R.B.S.A.	(266)	Gleaners Resting
	L.A.	(75)	The Ice Cart
	L.A.	(82)	A Welsh Peasant Girl at a Spring
	L.A.	(324)	Scene in Wales
	L.A.	(424)	Mending the Net
1843	R.A.	(715)	The Fisherman's Daughter *probably a miniature
	B.I.	(347)	The Hampshire Farmer – Home Brew'd Ale; 46 by 54 in
	B.I.	(356)	Cornish Market, People on the Beach; 46 by 54 in
	S.B.A.	(14)	Beach Scene with Figures
	S.B.A.	(35)	Fern-Cutters; 15 by 24 in; A.U.P. bt. John Floris Esq.; engraved
	S.B.A.	(181)	The Prawn-Fisher
	S.B.A.	(211)	A Village Festival; 40 by 60 in; bt. pt. A.U.P. G. S. Marshall; engraved; in the Tate Gallery Collection
	S.B.A.	(327)	The Goatherd
	S.B.A.	(430)	Waiting for the Mackerel-boats
	S.B.A.	(478)	Itinerent Fishmonger; 20 by 24 in; bt. pt. A.U.P. J. Holiday Esq.; engraved
	S.B.A.	(481)	Fisherman's Children; A.U.P. bt. R. McGlew
	S.B.A.	(494)	Devonshire Market Girls
	S.B.A.	(556)	Cattle – Evening
	S.B.A.	(572)	The Travelling Tinker
	S.B.A.	(576)	The Cowherd; 36 by 24 in; bt. pt. A.U.P. J. H. Strange Esq.; engraved
	R.M.I.	(4)	Beach Scene – Morning; sold
	R.M.I.	(137)	Market People on the Beach awaiting the Tide; bt. James Billhouses Esq.
	R.B.S.A.	(299)	The Travelling Tinker
	L.A.	(386)	The Prawn Fisher
	L.A.	(420)	Devonshire Market Girls

1844	B.I.	(400)	Finishing the Day's Sport; 53 by 65 in
	B.I.	(413)	Morning on the Beach; 53 by 65 in
	S.B.A.	(46)	Higglers
	S.B.A.	(115)	The Sand-Hill; 42 by 34 in; bt. pt. A.U.P. E. H. Braby Esq.; engraved
	S.B.A.	(159)	Gipsy Camp; sold pt. A.U.P.
	S.B.A.	(185)	Solitude; 46 by 28 in; bt. pt. A.U.P. Dr Jefferson; engraved
	S.B.A.	(203)	Poulterers Preparing for Market; 30 by 21 in; A.U.P. W. S. Potter Esq.; engraved
	S.B.A.	(232)	Beach Scene with Figures; 34 by 22 in; bt. pt. A.U.P. G. Miles Esq.; engraved
	S.B.A.	(279)	Fisherman's Children
	S.B.A.	(293)	The Dairy; 43 by 68 in; bt. pt. A.U.P. G. Reed Esq.; engraved
	S.B.A.	(380)	The Woodman's Dinner
	S.B.A.	(595)	Cattle and Figures – Evening Effect; sold A.U.P.
	R.M.I.	(4)	Beach Scene – Morning
	R.M.I.	(137)	Market People on the Beach Awaiting the Tide; sold James Billhouses Esq.
	R.B.S.A.	(77)	Fishermen's Children
	R.B.S.A.	(260)	The Woodman's Dinner
1845	B.I.	(466)	Rustic Conversation; 40 by 51 in
	B.I.	(502)	Cottage Scene, New Forest, Hants; 40 by 51 in
	S.B.A.	(68)	Pedlars Camp; sold pt. A.U.P.
	S.B.A.	(130)	Cattle and Figures by the Side of a River – Evening; 40 by 30 in; bt. pt. A.U.P. A. Dawson; engraved
	S.B.A.	(175)	The Gipsies' Retreat; 36 by 28 in; bt. A.U.P. W. Howlett Esq.; engraved
	S.B.A.	(281)	The Orphans
	S.B.A.	(312)	A Group from Nature
	S.B.A.	(386)	Waiting for the Ferry-Boat
	S.B.A.	(398)	The Rabbit-Man; bt. pt. A.U.P.
	S.B.A.	(471)	The Gleaners; 36 by 28 in; bt. pt. A.U.P. W. H. Bray Esq.; engraved
	S.B.A.	(570)	The Dairy Farm; sold A.U.P.
	S.B.A.	(599)	Returning from Pasture
	S.B.A.	(624)	The Return Waggon; 24 by 18 in; bt. pt. A.U.P. T. M. Daughty Esq.; engraved
	R.M.I.	(231)	The Cow Boy
	R.M.I.	(243)	A Gypsy Camp; sold
	R.M.I.	(528)	Morning on the Beach – Scene near Cornwall; sold
	R.M.I.	(545)	The Roadside Inn; sold
	R.B.S.A.	(13)	Rustic Figures; sold
	R.B.S.A.	(256)	Scene in Cornwall – Buying Fish; sold

	R.B.S.A.	(290)	Gypsy Mother; sold
	L.A.	(201)	Gipsies Pitching their Tent; sold
	L.A.	(203)	Cattle at the Brook; sold
	L.A.	(338)	Landscape and Cattle; sold
1846	B.I.	(397)	A Gipsy Family; 37 by 47 in; bt. A.U.P.
	B.I.	(424)	The Mountain Maid; 38 by 46 in; bt. pt. A.U.P. J. Faulkner Esq.; Bath; engraved
	S.B.A.	(19)	Gleanings at Netley, Hants; bt. pt. A.U.P.
	S.B.A.	(66)	Girl with Cattle; 20 by 24 in; bt. pt. A.U.P. H. S. Styan Esq., Bloomsbury; engraved
	S.B.A.	(135)	Harvest-Field – Dinner-Time
	S.B.A.	(226)	The Juvenile Gipsies; bt. pt. A.U.P.
	S.B.A.	(328)	Summer Evening – Returning Homeward; 45 by 32 in; bt. pt. A.U.P. H. E. Jordan Esq., Reading; engraved
	S.B.A.	(379)	The Pump; 24 by 32 in; bt. A.U.P. F. W. C. Reed Esq.; engraved
	S.B.A.	(414)	The Milk-Maid; 20 by 24 in; bt. A.U.P. W. H. Young Esq., High Holborn; engraved
	S.B.A.	(418)	Gipsies on the Skirts of the New Forest; bt. pt. A.U.P.
	S.B.A.	(490)	Gipsy Sisters
	S.B.A.	(507)	Shrimp-Girl – Coast of Cornwall
	S.B.A.	(562)	Rustic Figures with Cattle; 30 by 44 in; bt. A.U.P. F. Venning
	R.M.I.	(27)	Pedlars Halting
	R.M.I.	(98)	Girl with Cattle
	R.M.I.	(539)	Group of Gipsies
	R.B.S.A.	(9)	Gypsy Children
	R.B.S.A.	(128)	Cattle at a Brook
	R.B.S.A.	(298)	Loitering
	L.A.	(69)	Cattle in a Landscape
	L.A.	(197)	The Cow Boy
	L.A.	(198)	A Summer Evening
1847	B.I.	(473)	Travellers Resting; 40 by 50 in; sold A.U.P.
	B.I.	(498)	The Farm, Scene near Eusbury, Dorsetshire; 40 by 50 in; sold A.U.P.
	S.B.A.	(122)	The Wayside – Evening; sold A.U.P.
	S.B.A.	(168)	View from Stoney Cross, New Forest; sold A.U.P.
	S.B.A.	(296)	Harvest Time; sold A.U.P.
	S.B.A.	(309)	A Peasant Boy Driving Cattle
	S.B.A.	(360)	Interior of a Cow House; sold A.U.P.
	S.B.A.	(401)	Scene near Appledore, North Devon; sold A.U.P.
	S.B.A.	(413)	Tired Travellers; sold A.U.P.
	S.B.A.	(444)	Pedlars; sold A.U.P.

1847	S.B.A.	(449)	A Rustic with Cows; sold A.U.P.
(*contd.*)	S.B.A.	(476)	Returning from the Beach; sold A.U.P.
	S.B.A.	(494)	A Cottage Girl with Cattle; sold A.U.P.
	S.B.A.	(563)	The First Venture; sold A.U.P.
	R.M.I.	(160)	Girl with Cattle
	R.M.I.	(252)	On the Sussex Coast – Near Hastings
	R.M.I.	(338)	Tired Companion
	R.M.I.	(516)	A Cottage Door
	R.B.S.A.	(133)	Scene in North Devon
	R.B.S.A.	(191)	The Refreshing Draught; sold
	R.B.S.A.	(201)	A Shady Spot
	R.B.S.A.	(214)	The Young Gypsy
	R.B.S.A.	(429)	Cottage Girl and Cattle
	L.A.	(86)	The Plough Team
	L.A.	(176)	A Cow Shed
	L.A.	(232)	The Carriers Cart
	L.A.	(282)	In the Lanes at Millbrook, Hants
	L.A.	(356)	Lane Scene with Figures
1848	B.I.	(436)	A Shady Brook; 41 by 36 in
	B.I.	(499)	Devonshire Peasants; 41 by 36 in
	S.B.A.	(76)	Devonshire Scenery – Travellers Halting
	S.B.A.	(156)	A Bye-Lane, New Forest
	S.B.A.	(319)	The Pedlar; sold A.U.P.
	S.B.A.	(325)	The Farm
	S.B.A.	(330)	The Halfway House
	S.B.A.	(392)	Gipsy Girl and Donkey
	S.B.A.	(425)	In the Lanes near Portswood, Hants
	S.B.A.	(429)	Market-People returning Homeward
	S.B.A.	(443)	Rustic Figures
	S.B.A.	(513)	Girl with Cattle
	S.B.A.	(532)	The Plough Team; sold A.U.P.
	S.B.A.	(589)	Beach Scene, Isle of Wight; sold A.U.P.
	R.M.I.	(7)	Halt of Travellers
	R.M.I.	(200)	A Gipsy Tent
	R.M.I.	(385)	The Road-side Inn
	R.B.S.A.	(123)	Rustic Figures
	R.B.S.A.	(276)	The Pedlar
	R.B.S.A.	(396)	Devonshire Scenery – Travellers Halting
1849	B.I.	(438)	Itinerant Fishmonger; 36 by 36 in; sold
	B.I.	(444)	Scene on the Moors, Devonshire; 36 by 36 in; sold
	S.B.A.	(30)	The Gipsy Mother
	S.B.A.	(56)	Going to the Meadows
	S.B.A.	(114)	Looking out for the Fishing Boats – Coast of Sussex

	S.B.A.	(228)	Near the Deer Leap, New Forest
	S.B.A.	(264)	Autumnal Evening – Returning Homeward
	S.B.A.	(290)	Undercliff, Isle of Wight; sold A.U.P.
	S.B.A.	(344)	A Cottage Girl with Cattle
	S.B.A.	(364)	The Corn Field
	S.B.A.	(393)	Stable Friends
			*two well fed draught horses and goats
	S.B.A.	(411)	A Shady Glen
	S.B.A.	(457)	The Dairy Maid
	S.B.A.	(477)	Wood Scene, with Cattle and Figures; sold A.U.P.
	R.M.I.	(53)	Resting on the Way
	R.M.I.	(208)	Cattle – Evening
	R.M.I.	(326)	Scene near Rye – Sussex
	R.M.I.	(562)	Returning from Labour
	R.B.S.A.	(263)	Looking Out for the Fishing Boats
	R.B.S.A.	(416)	The Gipsy Mother
1850	B.I.	(222)	Girls with Cattle; 35 by 40 in
	B.I.	(234)	Group of Gipsies; 39 by 34 in
	S.B.A.	(105)	Pedlars in the New Forest
	S.B.A.	(149)	The Country Inn; sold A.U.P.
	S.B.A.	(162)	The Cornfield
	S.B.A.	(163)	Cattle and Figures – Evening
	S.B.A.	(215)	The Timber Waggon
	S.B.A.	(255)	On the Moors, Devonshire
	S.B.A.	(370)	Preparing the Meal
	S.B.A.	(387)	On the Beach near Puckester, Isle of Wight
	S.B.A.	(406)	A Cottage Door
	S.B.A.	(450)	Watering Cattle
	S.B.A.	(496)	A Gipsy Family; sold A.U.P.
	R.M.I.	(21)	Forest Shade
	R.M.I.	(100)	Part of the Ruins of Netley Abbey – Hants
	R.M.I.	(222)	A Gipsy Family
	R.M.I.	(409)	Group of Gipsies
	W.S.A.F.A.	(35)	Beach Scene, Isle of Wight
	W.S.A.F.A.	(73)	Landscape and Cattle, Devonshire; bt. by the Committee of the Art Union of Glasgow as a prize
	W.S.A.F.A.	(99)	New Forest, Hants
	W.S.A.F.A.	(113)	Cornfield near Ventnor, Isle of Wight
	W.S.A.F.A.	(194)	Resting by the Wayside; bt. by the Committee of the Art Union of Glasgow as a prize
	W.S.A.F.A.	(203)	Gleaners
1851	B.I.	(87)	Interior of a Cow shed; 20 by 22 in
	B.I.	(102)	The Ploughman's Meal; 20 by 22 in
	S.B.A.	(55)	Landscape and Cattle – Midday; bt. pt. A.U.P.

1851	S.B.A.	(89)	The Rabbit Seller; sold A.U.P.
(*contd.*)	S.B.A.	(135)	The Ale House; bt. pt. A.U.P.
	S.B.A.	(155)	Near Fordingbridge, Hants
	S.B.A.	(183)	Selsea Beach – Low Water
	S.B.A.	(231)	Morning on the Beach
	S.B.A.	(264)	Scene in the Lanes near Niton, Isle of Wight; sold A.U.P.
	S.B.A.	(277)	The Timber Waggon; sold A.U.P.
	S.B.A.	(451)	The Ploughman's Dinner
	S.B.A.	(465)	The Gipsy's Home
	S.B.A.	(468)	The Resting Place
	R.M.I.	(52)	The Gipsy Mother
	R.M.I.	(227)	The Gamekeeper's Return
	R.M.I.	(390)	The Pedlars' Camp
	W.S.A.F.A.	(148)	The Road Waggon
	W.S.A.F.A.	(221)	Preparing for Market
	W.S.A.F.A.	(235)	The Gipsy Family
1852	B.I.	(39)	Tired Pedlars; 36 by 42 in
	B.I.	(150)	A Gipsy Tent; 36 by 41 in
	S.B.A.	(93)	The Plough Team; sold A.U.P.
	S.B.A.	(109)	The Road Waggon; sold A.U.P.
	S.B.A.	(217)	Coast Scene – Morning
	S.B.A.	(296)	Group of Gipsies
	S.B.A.	(309)	Forest Shade; sold A.U.P.
	S.B.A.	(378)	The Village Inn
	S.B.A.	(434)	Forest Scene, with Gipsies
	S.B.A.	(489)	The Harvest Field; sold A.U.P.
	R.M.I.	(217)	Group of Rustics on Durley Common – Hants
	R.M.I.	(338)	Gipsies Halting
1853	S.B.A.	(34)	Forest Scene, with Cattle
	S.B.A.	(124)	Sand Boys – Scene on Durley Heath, Hants; sold A.U.P.
	S.B.A.	(158)	A Gipsy's Tent
	S.B.A.	(216)	Cornish Fishermen
	S.B.A.	(249)	The Corn Field
	S.B.A.	(282)	Village Ale-House – Drovers Halting
	S.B.A.	(462)	The Early Meal; sold A.U.P.
			*an unyoked team of plough horses with figures
	S.B.A.	(498)	Cattle and Figures – Evening; sold A.U.P.
1854	S.B.A.	(34)	Preparing the Mackerel Nets
	S.B.A.	(197)	Clovelly Pier, North Devon; sold A.U.P.
	S.B.A.	(242)	On the Banks of the Itchen, near Wood Mills
			*features a herd of cows
	S.B.A.	(344)	Wayside Chat

	S.B.A.	(356)	Gipsy's Camp, Evening
	S.B.A.	(455)	Wayfarers – Scene in the New Forest
	S.B.A.	(513)	A Dairy Cottage
1855	B.I.	(144)	A Cornish Fisherman
	B.I.	(293)	A Cottage Door
	S.B.A.	(186)	Finishing the Day's Sport
	S.B.A.	(238)	The Prawn Fisher
	S.B.A.	(319)	On the Banks, near Redbridge, Hampshire
	S.B.A.	(336)	On the Coast, near Clovelly, North Devon
	S.B.A.	(391)	Village Gossips
	S.B.A.	(453)	Rustics with Cattle – Evening
	S.B.A.	(496)	Travellers Reposing
	S.B.A.	(513)	The Gipsy's Haunt – Scene, New Forest
	R.M.I.	(60)	Rustics
	R.M.I.	(71)	Timber Waggon – Scene in the New Forest
	R.M.I.	(348)	On the Beach at Hastings
1856	B.I.	(82)	Gipsy Girls
	B.I.	(170)	Figures on the Beach, Evening
	S.B.A.	(73)	The Harvest Field
	S.B.A.	(81)	Rustic Figures
	S.B.A.	(200)	Woodlands in the New Forest, Hants
	S.B.A.	(249)	Cattle and Figures – Evening
	S.B.A.	(255)	Gleaners Resting
	S.B.A.	(329)	The Fish Stall
	S.B.A.	(458)	An Ale House Door
	S.B.A.	(502)	On the Banks of the Itchen
1857	S.B.A.	(38)	On the Beach, near Hastings
	S.B.A.	(166)	A Devonshire Fisherman and Grandchildren
	S.B.A.	(215)	The Prawn Fisher; sold A.U.P.
	S.B.A.	(373)	The Gipsy Camp; sold A.U.P.
	S.B.A.	(454)	The Borders of the New Forest
	S.B.A.	(469)	A Country Ale House; bt. pt. A.U.P.
	S.B.A.	(534)	The Rabbit Boy
	S.B.A.	(605)	Rustic Group – Autumnal Evening
	R.M.I.	(177)	A Bit, near Poole
	R.M.I.	(255)	Pedlars
	R.M.I.	(268)	Mending the Net
1858	B.I.	(410)	A Cottage Door
	B.I.	(474)	Welsh Peasants, Autumnal Evening
	S.B.A.	(138)	Near Lyndhurst, Hants
	S.B.A.	(166)	Coast Scene with Figures, North Devon
	S.B.A.	(174)	Young Gipsies
	S.B.A.	(176)	Figures on the Beach

1858	S.B.A.	(255)	Cornfield with Gleaners, Netley, Hants
	S.B.A.	(503)	A Lane in the New Forest
	S.B.A.	(522)	Group of Gipsies
	S.B.A.	(618)	Hastings Fisherman
	R.M.I.	(179)	The Timber Waggon – Scene in the New Forest
	R.M.I.	(237)	Gipsy Girls
	R.M.I.	(268)	On the Sussex Coast
	R.B.S.A.	(108)	Gleaners Resting
	R.B.S.A.	(207)	On the Dorset Coast
	R.B.S.A.	(226)	Village Pastime
1859	B.I.	(225)	Welsh Peasants
	B.I.	(240)	The Gipsy Mother
	B.I.	(418)	On the Beach near Hastings
	S.B.A.	(77)	Beach Scene – South Coast
	S.B.A.	(172)	On the Beach, near Hastings
	S.B.A.	(282)	The Dairy Cottage
	S.B.A.	(368)	Green Hill Lane, New Forest
	S.B.A.	(444)	The Way through the Fields
	S.B.A.	(457)	The Pet Donkey
	S.B.A.	(523)	Gipsy Group, New Forest
	S.B.A.	(572)	Part of the ruins of Netley Abbey
	R.B.S.A.	(150)	Loitering
	R.B.S.A.	(180)	Lane Scene, Isle of Wight
	R.B.S.A.	(518)	Rustic Figures
1860	B.I.	(237)	A Fisherman's Family
	B.I.	(594)	The Woodman
	S.B.A.	(133)	A Rest by the Way
	S.B.A.	(168)	Gipsy Camp, New Forest
	S.B.A.	(229)	Lane Scene, Isle of Wight
	S.B.A.	(268)	Fisherman's Cottage Door
	S.B.A.	(337)	Shrimpers on the South Coast
	S.B.A.	(456)	Village Girls, Gathering Fern
	S.B.A.	(608)	Autumnal Evening
	S.B.A.	(618)	Gipsies
	R.B.S.A.	(216)	Rustic Figures
	R.B.S.A.	(382)	A Fisherman's Family
1861	S.B.A.	(101)	Gleaners
	S.B.A.	(145)	Mending the Net
	S.B.A.	(158)	In the Lanes, near Broadlands, Hants
	S.B.A.	(191)	Going to the Meadows – Morning
	S.B.A.	(299)	An Ale-house Door
	S.B.A.	(400)	Gipsy Group; sold A.U.P.
	S.B.A.	(510)	Pedlars
	S.B.A.	(566)	Gipsy Family

1861	R.M.I.	(744)	In the Lanes, near Broadlands, Hants
	R.M.I.	(918)	Gipsy Family
	R.B.S.A.	(4)	Pedlars
	R.B.S.A.	(401)	An Ale-House Door
1862	B.I.	(222)	An Ale-house Door
	S.B.A.	(235)	Carting Timber in the New Forest; sold A.U.P.
	S.B.A.	(278)	Gamekeepers
	S.B.A.	(442)	Harvest Time
	S.B.A.	(466)	A Welsh Girl at a Spring
	S.B.A.	(585)	Cottagers; sold A.U.P.
	S.B.A.	(589)	The Cobbler
	S.B.A.	(618)	A Fisherman's Hut
	S.B.A.	(682)	The Reapers' Luncheon
1863	S.B.A.	(13)	A Dairyman's Cottage, near Lyndhurst, Hants
	S.B.A.	(153)	Fish Hawkers
	S.B.A.	(240)	On the Borders of the New Forest, Hants
	S.B.A.	(288)	Gipsy Camp
	S.B.A.	(304)	Autumnal Evening
	S.B.A.	(512)	The Cornfield; sold A.U.P.
	S.B.A.	(520)	Pedlars
	R.M.I.	(169)	Pedlars
	R.M.I.	(178)	Autumnal Evening
	R.M.I.	(589)	Fish Hawkers
	R.B.S.A.	(53)	Shrimpers on the South Coast
	R.B.S.A.	(91)	Rustic Figures
	R.B.S.A.	(93)	Beach Scene, with Figures
	R.B.S.A.	(592)	Fish Hawkers
	R.G.I.F.A.	(241)	Beach Scene, North Devon
	R.G.I.F.A.	(248)	A Gipsy Family – a Scene in the New Forest
	R.G.I.F.A.	(570)	A Group of Gipsies
	R.G.I.F.A.	(835)	On the Beach near Hastings
1864	S.B.A.	(48)	Pedlars Halting
	S.B.A.	(120)	Beach Scene – Evening
	S.B.A.	(130)	Market Folk on the Beach, North Devon
	S.B.A.	(194)	Scene on Durley Common
	S.B.A.	(198)	A Beach Scene
	S.B.A.	(267)	A Gipsy Family
	S.B.A.	(381)	Rustic Figures
	S.B.A.	(766)	Return from Market
1865	S.B.A.	(241)	A Scene in Harvest
	S.B.A.	(263)	Gipsy Girls
	S.B.A.	(281)	The Cornfield – Midday
	S.B.A.	(486)	Gipsy Family
	S.B.A.	(560)	Waiting for the Fishboats

1865	S.B.A.	(592)	Scene in the Isle of Wight
(contd.)	S.B.A.	(627)	A Farm Labourer Resting
	S.B.A.	(688)	Gleaners at the Stile
	R.M.I.	(674)	Interior of a Stable
1866	S.B.A.	(48)	Fish Hawkers
	S.B.A.	(275)	Gipsy Girls; sold A.U.P.
	S.B.A.	(319)	The Fisherman's Leisure Hour
	S.B.A.	(361)	Gleaners; sold A.U.P.
	S.B.A.	(389)	Shrimpers
	S.B.A.	(490)	The Cornfield
	S.B.A.	(509)	Morning on the Beach, North Devon
1867	S.B.A.	(199)	Bargaining for Fish
	S.B.A.	(256)	A Gipsy Family
	S.B.A.	(330)	Evening on the Beach – Mending the Net
	S.B.A.	(406)	Preparing for Market
	S.B.A.	(463)	The Carrier's Cart: A Vale in the New Forest: The Isle of Wight and Needle Rocks in the Distance
	S.B.A.	(604)	Tasting the October Brewing
	R.G.I.F.A.	(118)	Loitering
	R.G.I.F.A.	(527)	Rustic Figures
1868	S.B.A.	(17)	The Ploughman's Dinner; sold A.U.P.
	S.B.A.	(272)	The Gipsy's Home
	S.B.A.	(307)	Gathering Fern
	S.B.A.	(493)	A Gipsy Family – Evening; sold A.U.P.
	S.B.A.	(499)	Returning from the Beach
	S.B.A.	(534)	East Window of Netley Abbey
	S.B.A.	(603)	Gipsy's Tent
1869	S.B.A.	(215)	Fish Hawkers
	S.B.A.	(256)	Morning in the Meadows
	S.B.A.	(384)	On the Beach
	S.B.A.	(475)	A Fish Stall
	S.B.A.	(496)	The Cornfield – Reapers Resting
	R.M.I.	(596)	The Keeper's Cottage Door
1870	S.B.A.	(127)	Gleaners
	S.B.A.	(141)	The Morning Lesson
	S.B.A.	(423)	Poultry Hawkers Preparing for Market

WILLIAM JOSEPH SHAYER

1828	H.P.G.	(–)	Portrait of a Mare
1829	S.B.A.	(287)	Trout, from Nature
	H.P.G.	(–)	Foxes after Landseer
	H.P.G.	(–)	Lobster and Mackerel

	H.P.G.	(–)	Dogs and Company
	H.P.G.	(–)	Pigs
1841	B.I.	(315)	Greyhounds; 22 by 26 in
	S.B.A.	(653)	A Favourite Horse
1844	S.B.A.	(89)	Copenhagen, a Favourite Charger, the property of His Grace the Duke of Wellington
	S.B.A.	(105)	Adeliza, a Roan Heifer, the property of Josh. Phillips Esq. of Ardington, Berks
	S.B.A.	(162)	Portrait of Poison, Winner of the Oaks Stakes, at Epsom 1843
1845	S.B.A.	(103)	A Favourite Horse, the property of Capt. R. Howard Vyne, of the Royal Horse Guards
	S.B.A.	(297)	A Park Horse, the property of a Lady
1848	S.B.A.	(405)	Major, Bounce and Rap, three Setters, the property of ? Horsley Esq.
1849	S.B.A.	(139)	The Shooting Pony
	S.B.A.	(247)	The Farm Stable
1853	S.B.A.	(426)	Country Inn
1855	S.B.A.	(435)	Portrait of Autocrat, the property of R. E. Cooper Esq.
1858	R.A.	(697)	Doing it Cleverly
	S.B.A.	(79)	The 1st of September
	S.B.A.	(209)	The 1st of October
	S.B.A.	(518)	A Way They Have in Leicestershire
1859	S.B.A.	(487)	Landscape and Cattle, Earlswood Common, Red Hill, Surrey
	S.B.A.	(491)	Crossing the Brook – the Bay Refuses
	S.B.A.	(608)	A Bright Day, Gipsies Shifting Quarters, Earlswood Common
1860	S.B.A.	(626)	Eton from the Thames
1861	R.M.I.	(249)	Hunting – Full Cry
	R.M.I.	(704)	Gipsies Shifting Quarters – Earlswood Common, Surrey
	R.M.I.	(–)	Flower Girl
1885	R.A.	(1010)	Leisure Moments

CHARLES SHAYER

| 1879 | S.B.A. | (472) | An Interior of a Stable |

CHAPTER TEN
Sale of Remaining Works
by William Shayer 1881

The remaining works by William Shayer senior were sold by Henry Shayer. The sale was held by Messrs. Christie, Manson and Woods on Saturday, 19th March 1881, at 8 King Street, St. James's Square, London. The works of William Shayer senior began at lot number 296.

296 A Roosting Place – from Nature
297 A Child Blowing Bubbles
298 Pack Donkeys
299 A Carpenter
300 A Boy at a Well
301 Dairy Farm, near Brixham
302 A Landscape, with Peasants and Cows
303 A Mountain Scene
304 A Devonshire Gamekeeper
305 Gipsies
306 The Reaper Resting
307 Will You Buy?
308 A Devonshire Pack-horse
309 Cutting Timber
310 An Old Lime-Kiln, near Clovelly
311 A Coast Scene, with Fisherman and Children
312 The Archway, Clovelly
313 The Boroughs, North Devon
314 A Landscape, with a Peasant and Cattle
315 Cottages at Clovelly
316 On the Coast
317 Prawn Fishers
318 A Coast Scene, with Old Jetty, Fishermen, and Donkeys
319 Fishing Boats off the Coast
320 Interior, with a Woman Washing
321 A River Scene, with Boy on Grey Pony, Peasants, and Cattle
322 The Rabbit-Seller
323 Clovelly Pier from the Heights
324 The Gipsy's Home
325 Bargaining for Fish on the Beach
326 The Fish-Stall
327 Preparing for Market
328 Wreckers: Storm Clearing Off

CHAPTER ELEVEN
Sale of Works
by Charles Waller Shayer 1894

A sale of paintings by Charles Shayer was held by Messrs. Foster on Wednesday, 31st October 1894 at 54 Pall Mall, London.

145 A Lane Scene
146 A Village Inn
147 A Farm Yard
148 A Village Smithy
149 Returning from Market
150 A Meadow Scene

List of Works by the Shayer Family in the Public Galleries of Great Britain

The following is an alphabetical list of towns and cities in Great Britain with galleries possessing works by members of the Shayer family. Due to the large number of these galleries it has mostly been necessary to rely on the details and attributions kindly provided by the galleries themselves. The work of the Shayer family and their followers can be easily confused, and so it is possible that some of these attributions may be mistaken. Nevertheless it is hoped that this list will prove useful, and anyone wishing to view any of these works is strongly advised to enquire in advance whether the work is on display or available for viewing.

ACCRINGTON (Lancashire)
Haworth Art Gallery, Haworth Park
William Shayer
Coastal Scene with Figures
signed and dated 1852
38 by 52 in

William Shayer
Harvest Time
signed and dated 1855
24 by 20 in

ARUNDEL (West Sussex)
Arundel Castle
attributed to William Joseph Shayer
Children Playing in a Village Street
$8\frac{5}{8}$ by $11\frac{5}{8}$ in
on panel

BARNSLEY (South Yorkshire)
Cooper Art Gallery, Church Street
William Shayer
Landscape with Cattle
30 by 25 in

BARNSTAPLE (Devon)
The North Devon Athenaeum, The Square
William Shayer
Beach Scene
signed and dated 1841
30 by 38 in
Provenance Mr Pook, Taw Vale Brewery

BIDEFORD (Devon)
Burton Art Gallery, Victoria Park, Kingsley Road
William Shayer
The Stable
$35\frac{1}{4}$ by $35\frac{1}{4}$ in
Donated by Thomas Burton 1954

William Shayer
The Travellers
30 by 24 in
Donated by Thomas Burton 1954

BLACKPOOL (Lancashire)
Grundy Art Gallery, Queen Street
William Joseph Shayer
Cattle
49 by 38 in

William Shayer
Fisherfolk
77 by 55 in

BRISTOL
City of Bristol Art Gallery, Queen's Road, Bristol 8
William Shayer
Timber Hauling
signed
30 by 40 in
Bequest of Miss E. G. Atkins 1930

BURNLEY (Lancashire)
Towneley Hall Art Gallery and Museum
William Shayer
A Woodside Inn
signed and dated 1841
17 by 23 in
Purchased 1950 from Mr R. H. Spurr,
   Southport

CALDERDALE (West Yorkshire)
Bankfield Museum and Art Gallery,
   Akroyd Park, Halifax
William Shayer
A Gipsy Encampment
28 by 35¾ in
Presented by Alderman William Smith
   1907

William Shayer
Harvesting
8¼ by 12¼ in

William Shayer
Returning from Market
12¼ by 14 in
Donated by Alderman William Smith
   1907

CAMBRIDGE
Anglesey Abbey, Lode
William Joseph Shayer
Match between Mr T. Crosby's 'Copper
   Captain' and Lord Lichfield's 'Minster', October 1833
signed and dated 1833
16¾ by 21 in
on panel

CAMBRIDGE
Fitzwilliam Museum, Trumpington
   Street
William Shayer
The Prawn Fishers
signed
24 by 29⅞ in
Bequest of Samuel Sandars (1837–1894)

CHELTENHAM (Gloucestershire)
Cheltenham Art Gallery and Museum,
   Clarence Street
William Shayer
Cottage Door
signed and dated 1847
201⁄16 by 24 in
Donated by G. G. Brodie 1927

William Shayer
Coast Scene with Fisherfolk
signed
24⅞ by 36⅝ in
Acquired from Exors. of Thos. Rishworth. See Rishworth Catalogue no.
   86

William Shayer
The Milkmaid
signed and dated 1840
30 by 25 in
Acquired from Exors. of Thos. Rishworth 1953. See Rishworth Catalogue
   no. 87

William Shayer
Interior of a Fisherman's Cottage
signed
13⅞ by 18 in
Exhibited 1937; Victorian Exhibition
   City of Birmingham Museum and Art
   Gallery
Acquired from Exors. of Thos. Rish-
   worth 1953. See Rishworth Catalogue
   no. 88

William Shayer
Gipsy Encampment – Man with a White
   Horse
24⅛ by 20 in
Acquired from Exors. of Thos. Rishworth 1953. Not in Rishworth Catalogue

William Shayer
Fisherman Mending His Nets
signed and indistinctly dated 184–
29⅞ by 35⅞ in
Donated by Sir Walter Craddock, Am-
   berley, Glos. 1963

CHICHESTER (West Sussex)
West Sussex Record Office, County Hall,
  Chichester
William Shayer
Portrait of the Three Smith Brothers
signed and dated 1811
17 by 24 in
Provenance: W. H. B. Fletcher. bt. Capt.
  A. W. Fuller; donated by Mrs Fuller
  in memory of her late husband
*The painting is copied from a print by
  William Pether (1731–1778), and was
  for some time considered to be the
  original painting by Pether, until
  cleaning revealed William Shayer's
  signature

DONCASTER (South Yorkshire)
Doncaster Museum and Art Gallery,
  Chequer Road
William Shayer
Figures on a Beach
signed
26½ by 36½ in
Robert Stockil Bequest

EASTBOURNE (East Sussex)
The Towner Art Gallery, Manor House,
  9 Borough Lane
William Shayer
Shore Scene with Figures
27¼ by 35½ in
Alderman John Chisholm Towner Be-
  quest 1919

EXETER (Devon)
Royal Albert Museum and Art Gallery,
  Queen Street
William Shayer
Landscape with Cattle, Horses and
  Figures
20 by 24 in
Lady Lockyer Bequest 1943

GLASGOW
City of Glasgow Art Gallery and Mus-
  eum, Kelvingrove
William Shayer
Landscape with Cattle
signed
13½ by 11½ in
On panel
Euing Collection

William Shayer
Landscape with Cattle
11¾ by 9½ in
Euing Collection

William Shayer
The Shrimp Girl, Cornish Coast
signed
27 by 35 in
Euing Collection

William Shayer
A Gipsy Encampment
23¼ by 19¼ in
Smellie Collection

William Shayer
A Woody Stream
signed and dated 1846
9¾ by 11½ in
On panel
The Eck Bequest 1915

William Shayer
Ploughing
signed and dated 1846
13¾ by 11¾ in
The Eck Bequest 1915

William Joseph Shayer
A Shady Pool
5¼ by 6¾ in
Millboard
Euing Collection

William Joseph Shayer: 'The Duke of Beaufort's Coach leaving the Bull and Mouth, Regent's Street'; signed and dated 1840; 18 by 24 in; photograph by courtesy of Richard Green Galleries, London.

William Joseph Shayer: 'A Coach and Four Ready to Go' (one of a set of four, see also plates 64, 65 and 66); signed and dated 1878; 13 by 20 in; photograph by courtesy of Richard Green Galleries, London.

Henry and Charles Shayer: 'A Farm Boy Watering Horses at a Village Pond' (one of a pair, see below); 12 by 16 in; photograph by courtesy of Richard Green Galleries, London.

Henry and Charles Shayer: 'A Farmyard Scene' (one of a pair, see above); 12 by 16 in; photograph by courtesy of Richard Green Galleries, London.

HASTINGS (East Sussex)
Hastings Museum and Art Gallery,
    Cambridge Road
Style of Shayer
Carthorses and Rustics by a Stream
bears signature and dated 1840
18½ by 35 in
Donated by Col. Hornblower of Etch-
    ingham

HUDDERSFIELD (West Yorkshire)
Huddersfield Art Gallery, Princess Alex-
    andra Walk
William Shayer
Coast Scene
signed and dated 1838
26¾ by 32 in
Donated by the Sykes family 1939

HULL (Humberside)
Ferens Art Gallery, Queen Victoria
    Square
William Shayer
Beach Scene
30 by 39⅞ in
Bequest of Alfred Jordan 1942

William Shayer
Coast Scene with Dutch Fishing Craft
signed and dated 1846
10⅛ by 14 in
On cardboard
Donated by Mrs T. W. Mackrill 1951

LEEDS (West Yorkshire)
City Art Gallery
William Shayer
Fisher Folk on the Shore
signed and dated 1839
33 by 42 in
Donated by Samuel Smith 1933

LEICESTER
The Leicestershire Museum and Art
    Gallery
William Shayer
The Timber Waggon
40 by 33 in
Purchased from Mr Palser, May 1883
Collection: N. S. Johnson, Christie's Sale
    5th May 1883 lot 94
Literature: Stella Walker *Sporting Art;
    England 1700–1900* page 84 plate 133

William Joseph Shayer
Coursing
signed and dated 1842
11¾ by 16 in
Purchased at Messrs. Christie's 1890
Collection: T. M. Whitehouse, Christie's
    Sale 29th March 1890 lot 48 as by T.
    Woodward of Worcester. The paint-
    ing was reattributed after subsequent
    cleaning revealed signature

Style of Shayer
At the Farm
bears signature and date 1840
15 by 19 in
Purchased from Messrs. Withers

LIVERPOOL (Merseyside)
The Walker Art Gallery, William Brown
    Street
William Shayer
Plinlimmon and the Sources of the Wye
40⅛ by 35⅛ in
Donated by Andrew P. Lusk 1928
Exhibited: similar frame and size to B.I.
    1834 (46)
Provenance: Adcote Hall, Shropshire;
    Russell, Woods and Sons, Hereford.
    An indistinct label reads ----- Wm
    Shayer/Southampton

LONDON
Guildhall Art Gallery
William Shayer
Harvest Time
signed
14 by 12 in
Bequeathed to Corporation of City of
    London by William Dunnett 1888
Exhibited R.B.A. 1923, Bradford 1930

William Shayer
Milking Time
signed
24 by 20 in
Purchased by the Corporation 1932
Literature: J. Maas *Victorian Painters*
    page 52

LONDON
The Tate Gallery, Millbank
William Shayer
A Village Festival
signed
$35\frac{1}{2}$ by $42\frac{3}{4}$ in
Presented by the executors of C. F.
    Dendy Marshall 1955
Exhibited: S.B.A. 1843 (211) Art Union
    Prize

John Crome and William Shayer
A View of Chapel-Fields, Norwich
29 by 41 in
Exhibited: possibly Norwich Society
    1820 (80)
Provenance: William Spratt, Norwich,
    a friend and patron of Crome; by
    descent to A. W. Spratt, his grandson;
    Henry F. Chorley, by whom it was
    bequeathed to the National Gallery,
    London; transferred to the Tate Gal-
    ery 1919
Etching by R. S. Chattock. Whereabouts
    unknown. Impressions reproduced in
    Standard 21st December 1885

Literature: various – a complete booklist
    appears in Norman L. Goldberg's
    John Crome the Elder (Oxford 1978)
    p. 227 catalogue no. 111
This painting was said to have reached
    A. W. Spratt in what he considered
    was an unfinished state, and the cattle
    and figures were added by William
    Shayer

LONDON
Victoria and Albert Museum, Cromwell
    Road, South Kensington
William Shayer
Buying Fish
$10\frac{1}{4}$ by 12 in
On panel
Townsend Bequest 1868

William Shayer
Coast Scene with Fishing Smacks and
    Groups of Fisherfolk
signed and dated 1841
$13\frac{1}{2}$ by $17\frac{1}{2}$ in
Provenance: bt. from E. Parson in
    Brompton 7th November 1887

MANCHESTER
The City Art Gallery, Mosley Street,
    Manchester
William Shayer
Landscape with Cattle by a Stream (also
    called Changing Pastures)
signed
$28\frac{1}{2}$ by $36\frac{1}{4}$ in
James Gresham Bequest

MERTHYR TYDFIL (Mid Glamorgan)
Art Gallery and Museum, Cyfarthfa Castle
William Shayer
Milking Time
29 by 24 in
Purchased 1911

NEWCASTLE UPON TYNE
Laing Art Gallery, Higham Place
William Shayer
Landscape with Cattle
24 by 20 in
Bequest of John Lamb 1909

William Shayer
Gypsy Encampment
16 by 24 in
Bequest of W. Wilson 1955

NEWPORT (Gwent)
Museum and Art Gallery, John Frost Square

William Shayer
Landscape with Cattle and Figure of a Woman
signed and dated 1842
20 by 24½ in
Local gift, accession no. 51-46.6

William Shayer
Pastoral Scene, Cattle and Figures
20 by 30 in
Local gift, accession no. 51-46.4

NOTTINGHAM
Nottingham Castle Museum
William Shayer
A Gypsy Encampment
39¼ by 34¼ in
Provenance: F.J. Nettlefold Collection. Bequeathed in 1948

Literature: C. Reginald Grundy and F. Gordon-Roe *A Catalogue of the Pictures and Drawings in the Collection of Frederick John Nettlefold* Volume III, 1937

OLDHAM (Greater Manchester)
Art Gallery and Museum, Union Street
William Shayer
Farmyard Scene
signed and dated 1841
30 by 40 in
Donated by Simon Holden 1960

Style of Shayer
Coast Scene with figures
bears signature and date 1846
20 by 36 in
Donated by C. E. Kidd 1957

PERTH
Perth Museum and Art Gallery, George Street
William Joseph Shayer and Edward Charles Williams
Landscape with Cows
signed by both artists
36 by 52 in

ROCHDALE (Greater Manchester)
Rochdale Art Gallery, Esplanade
William Shayer
Group of Gypsies
19⅞ by 24 in
Donated by C. Stott 1921

ROSSENDALE (Lancashire)
Rossendale Museum, Whitaker Park, Rawtenstall
William Shayer
Near Southampton – Gypsy Scene with Animals
signed
23½ by 28¾ in
Mrs Louisa Haine Bequest 1969

SALFORD (Greater Manchester)
Museum and Art Gallery, The Crescent,
  Peel Park
William Shayer
Landscape with Gypsy Figures
signed and dated 1846
28 by 35 in
Purchased from Messrs. Charles Nicholls
  & Son, Deansgate, Manchester

SHEFFIELD (South Yorkshire)
Mappin Art Gallery, Weston Park
William Shayer
Shore Scene
signed and dated 1841
$24\frac{1}{2}$ by $29\frac{1}{2}$ in

William Shayer
Coast Scene
$11\frac{1}{4}$ by $15\frac{1}{4}$ in
On millboard

William Shayer
The White Cow
signed and dated 1840
$11\frac{3}{4}$ by $13\frac{3}{4}$ in

William Shayer
Donkey and Sheep
12 by 15 in
On panel

William Shayer
Coast Scene
$25\frac{1}{2}$ by $35\frac{1}{2}$ in

William Shayer
Fisherman's Children
19 by $22\frac{3}{4}$ in

SOUTHAMPTON (Hampshire)
Southampton Art Gallery, Civic Centre
William Shayer
Coast Scene
signed
30 by $39\frac{1}{8}$ in
Smith Bequest 1926

William Shayer
Gypsies in the Wood
signed
$24\frac{1}{4}$ by 20 in
Provenance: purchased from Frank
  Kimber, Southampton. Chipperfield
  Bequest 1933

William Shayer
Milking Time
signed
28 by 36 in
Provenance: purchased from the Palser
  Gallery, London. Chipperfield Bequest 1933

William Shayer
The Fish Stall
signed
28 by $36\frac{1}{8}$ in
Donated by Miss E. M. Welch 1943

William Shayer
The Gleaners
signed, and signed and inscribed on an
  old label on the reverse
12 by 16 in
Donated by Miss E. M. Welch 1943

William Shayer
A Shady Corner
28 by 36 in
Provenance: Sir James Murray; donated
  by F. J. Nettlefold 1948
Literature: C. Reginald Grundy and F.
  Gordon-Roe *A Catalogue of the Paintings and Drawings in the Collection of Frederick John Nettlefold* Volume III 1937
*According to this catalogue the painting was signed and dated 1840. It was obviously removed by cleaning before it was presented to Southampton Art Gallery

William Shayer
Coast Scene
signed
28⅛ by 36⅛ in
Chipperfield Bequest 1911

William Shayer
Mouth of the Old Canal Platform
signed and dated 1812
11¾ by 17 in
William Burrough-Hill Bequest

Henry and Charles Shayer
The White Swan
signed
28 by 36½ in
Henry Glasspool Bequest 1947

Henry and Charles Shayer
Coast Scene with Figures and Boats and
   a Church
signed (also bears William Shayer's signature and date 1833)
14¼ by 18 in
Provenance: W. J. M. Smee, Esq. Presented from the Ernest E. Cook Collection through the National Art-
   Collections Fund

SOUTHPORT (Merseyside)
Atkinson Art Gallery, Lord Street
William Shayer
Fishermen
signed and dated '54
14 by 12 in
Donated by Mrs Gray, the widow of
   George Preston

William Shayer
Fisherwomen
signed and dated '54
14 by 12 in
Donated by Mrs Gray, the widow of
   George Preston

William Shayer
Coast Scene with Figures and Horses
signed
25 by 35 in
Donated by F. J. Nettlefold 1948
Literature: C. Reginald Grundy and F.
   Gordon-Roe *A Catalogue of the Paint-
   ings and Drawings in the Collection of
   Frederick John Nettlefold* Volume III
   1937
Reproduced as a greetings card by
   Parnassus Galleries 1979

STOKE-ON-TRENT (Staffordshire)
City Museum and Art Gallery, Broad
   Street, Hanley
William Shayer
The Blue Ball, North Devon
29 by 49 in

SUNDERLAND (Tyne and Wear)
Museum and Art Gallery, Borough Road
William Shayer
A Farmstead: Milking Time
signed
53 by 44 in
John Dickinson Bequest 1908

WALSALL (West Midlands)
Museum and Art Gallery, Lichfield
   Street
Style of William Shayer
Cows
10 by 12 in
Henry J. Thrustans Bequest 1932

Style of William Shayer
Landscape (Cattle at a stream)
bears signature and date 1865
30 by 25 in
Alderman C. C. Walker Bequest 1929

Style of William Shayer
Cows
11 by 14 in
Henry J. Thrustans Bequest 1932

Henry and Charles Shayer
Landscape with Figures and Donkeys
signed
20 by 23 in
Mr S. Drew Bequest 1922

Charles Shayer
Horse Fair
signed
26 by 44 in
Provenance: William Christie 1899

William Joseph Shayer and Charles
  Marshall
Ben Nevis and Mountain Stream
signed and dated 1855
41 by 55 in
Alderman C. C. Walker Bequest 1929

WOLVERHAMPTON (West Mid-
  lands
Central Art Gallery, Lichfield Street
William Shayer
The Gipsy Tent
30 by 25 in
Horsman Bequest 1886

William Shayer
Landscape with Boy and Donkey
14 by 11¾ in
On panel
Paul Lutz Bequest 1899

William Shayer
On the Beach at Portishead
14 by 18 in
Donated by Mrs Gilbert 1945

William Shayer
Landscape
18 by 24 in
Purchased Christie's 7th May 1954, ex
  Gaskell Collection lot 114

YORK (North Yorkshire)
York City Art Gallery, Exhibition
  Square
William Shayer
Milking Time
signed
24 by 19½ in
On panel
Provenance: I. Whitehead, York; Bur-
  ton Bequest 1882

Select Bibliography

Allentuck, M.   'Sir Uvedale Price and the Picturesque Garden: the Evidence of the Coleorton Papers' from *The Picturesque Garden and its influence outside the British Isles*, ed. Nikolaus Pevsner (Washington 1974)

Arlot, ?   *A Complete Guide for Coachpainters* (London 1871)

Barrell, J.   *The Dark Side of the Landscape* (Cambridge 1980)

Bénézet, E.   *Dictionnaire critique et documentaire des Peintres, Sculpteurs, Dessinateurs et Graveurs* (Paris 1954)

Blew, W. C.   *The Coaching Revival* (London 1889)

Bryan, M.   *Bryan's Dictionary of Painters and Engravers* (London 1905)

Burgess, J. W.   *Treatise on Coach Building* (London 1881)

Challen, W. H.   'Baldy's Garden, the Painters Lambert, and other Sussex Families' in *Sussex Archaeological Collections* Vol 90 (Oxford 1952)

Cobbett, W.   *Rural Rides* (London 1830)

Crawford, D. G.   *The History of the Indian Medical Service* (London 1914)

Cutten, M. J.   *Some Inns and Alehouses of Chichester* (Chichester 1964)

Cutten, M. J. and Steer, F. W.   *Changing Chichester* (Chichester 1961)

Day, H. A. E.   *East Anglian Painters* (Eastbourne 1967–69)

Falk, B.   *Five Years Dead* (London 1937)

Falk, B.   *Old Q's Daughter* (London 1937)

Fawcett, T.   *The Rise of English Provincial Art* (Oxford 1974)

Fitzroy, H. C. (the 8th Duke of Beaufort)   *Driving* (London 1890)

Francis, T.   *History of Freemasonry in Sussex* (Portsmouth 1883)

Frost and Reed   *Catalogue of Sporting Engravings* (London 1972)

Frost and Reed   *The Home Lover's Book* 23rd edition

Gilbey, W.   *Animal Painters* (London 1900)

Gilpin, W.   *Three Essays on Picturesque Beauty, on Picturesque Travel and on Sketching Landscape to which is added a poem on Landscape Painting* (London 1794)

Grant, M. H.   *Old English Landscape Painters* (Leigh-on-Sea 1947)

Graves, A.   *Exhibitors at the British Institution 1806–67* (London 1908)

Grego, J.   'Art Unions and Art Lotteries' from the *Magazine of Art* 1888

Grundy, C. Reginald and Roe, F. Gordon *A Catalogue of Pictures and Drawings in the Collection of Frederick John Nettleford* Vol III (London 1937)

Hearnshaw, F. J. C.   *Relics of Old Southampton* (Southampton 1904)

Hubbard, E. H.   *An Outline History of the Royal Society of British Artists 1823–40* (London 1937)

Hubbard, E. H.   *A Hundred Years of British Painting 1851–1951* (London 1951)

Hussey, C.   *The Picturesque* (London 1967)

Hyams, E.   *Capability Brown and Humphry Repton* (London 1971)

Kitson, S.   *The Life of John Sell Cotman* (London 1937)

Maas, J. *Victorian Painters* (London 1967)

McCausland, H. *Old Sporting Characters and Occasions from Sporting and Road History* (London 1948)

McCausland, H. *The English Carriage* (London 1948)

Mornington, G. 'The Very Peculiar Folk of St Mary Extra' in *Hampshire Magazine* Vol 17 no. 12, October 1977

Mullaly, T. 'The Three Smiths of Chichester' in *Sussex County Magazine* Vol 28 no. 2, February 1954

Noakes, A. *Sportsmen in Landscape* (London 1954)

Ottley, H. *Dictionary of Painters and Engravers* (London 1866)

Patterson, A. Temple *A History of Southampton* (Southampton 1966)

Peat, A. H. and Halstead, L. C. *Churches and Other Antiquities of West Sussex* (Chichester 1912)

Price, B. *Bygone Chichester* (Chichester 1975)

Price, U. *Essays on the Picturesque as compared with the Sublime and the Beautiful and on the Use of Studying Pictures for the Purpose of Improving landscape* (London 1794)

Pyne, W. H. *Picturesque Views of Rural Occupations* (London 1806)

Reynolds, J. *The Williams Family of Painters* (Woodbridge 1975)

Roe, F. Gordon *British Sporting Artists* (London 1922)

Roe, F. Gordon *Henry Bright of the Norwich School* (London 1920)

Rudall, J. *A Memoir of the Rev. James Crabb* (London 1854)

St Clair, J. *Old Chichester Lodges* (Chichester 1927)

Sartin, S. *Thomas Sidney Cooper* (Leigh-on-Sea 1976)

Siltzer, F. *The Story of British Sporting Prints* (London 1925)

Smith, C. J. 'Funeral Hatchments' in *The Amateur Historian* Vol 2 no. 5 April–May 1955

Sparrow, W. S. *British Sporting Artists* (London 1931)

Steer, F. W. 'Heraldic Coach Panels' in *Sussex County Magazine* Vol 29 no. 6, June 1955

Steer, F. W. *The Dolphin and Anchor Hotel* (Chichester 1961)

Turley, R. *A Survey of Hampshire and Isle of Wight Art exhibited in London c. 1760–1900* (Winchester 1978)

Tyne and Wear County Council Museum *Clarkson Stanfield* (Gateshead 1979)

Walker, S. *British Sporting Art* (London 1972)

Watson, K. L. 'All at Sea?' *The Manchester Genealogist* Spring edition 1975

Willis, T. G. *Records of Chichester* (Chichester 1928)

Wood, C. *Dictionary of Victorian Painters* (Woodbridge 1971)

Wood, C. *Victorian Panorama* (London 1976)

The Dictionary of National Biography (Oxford 1963–64)

The Black and White Plates

Of those examples here chosen to represent the range and general development of William Shayer's work, a few contain minor contributions by his sons, Henry and Charles Shayer. For example, in plate 47 'The Plough Team' it is evident that the sons assisted in the production of the background landscape. In this, and the other few cases illustrated, William Shayer has clearly 'put the picture in good order', and for this reason it was considered that the more complete attribution to 'William, Henry and Charles Shayer' could be misleading. The selection of illustrations attributed to William Shayer represent, therefore, work that was in the authors' opinion largely executed by his hand.

1 – William Shayer: 'Reform the Artist' (always known as 'The Poor Artist'); 4 by 3 in; pen and ink, and watercolour; private collection. (This amusing self-portrait always hung at the bottom of William Shayer's easel, see page 9.)

2 – William Shayer: 'Trompe l'oeil'; signed and dated 1809; 16½ by 20½ in; pen and ink, and water-colour; photograph by courtesy of the proprietors of the *Hampshire Chronicle*. (The *Hampshire Chronicle* Vol. XLII no. 1815 is dated 26th December 1808 and not, as it appears in Shayer's drawing, 1809, so it must be assumed that this was Shayer's ingenious means of dating his work. He probably kept the newspaper for an article on the removal of picture varnish which appeared in this issue.)

3 – Reputedly by William Shayer: 'The Coat of Arms of General Sir Edward Paget G.C.B.'; 11¼ by 14 in; part of coach panel; private collection.

4 – William Shayer: Portrait of the three Smith Brothers of Chichester after a print by William Pether; signed and dated 1811; 17 by 24 in; photograph by courtesy of the West Sussex Record Office.

5 – William Shayer: 'The Mouth of the Old Canal Platform, Southampton'; signed and dated 1812; 11¾ by 17 in; photograph by courtesy of Southampton Art Gallery.

6 – William Shayer: 'Travellers in a Wooded Landscape'; signed, dated and inscribed 'Southampton 1812'; 20 by 26 in; photograph by courtesy of Richard Green Galleries, London.

7 – William Shayer:
'The Engagement
of H.M.S.
Alexander
Commanded by
Sir Richard
Rodney Bligh with
a French Squadron
under Rear-
Admiral Neuilly of
Three Line of
Battle Shipps and
One Frigate' after
a print by Thomas
Guest; signed and
dated May 1819;
34 by 55 in; where-
abouts now unknown.
(See page 6.)

8 – William Shayer: 'The Return to the Farm'; signed and dated October 10 1821; 24 by 33 in; photograph by courtesy of Sotheby's.

9 – William Shayer: 'Rosslyn Castle'; 17 by 21 in; on panel; photograph by courtesy of Cooling Galleries Ltd, London.

10 – William Shayer: 'The Tired Gleaners'; signed and dated 1830; 27½ by 36 in; photograph by courtesy of Richard Green Galleries, London.

11 – William Shayer: 'The Gardener's Cottage, Alverstoke, Hampshire'; signed and dated 1835; 28 by 36 in; photograph by courtesy of the Leger Galleries Ltd, London.

12 – William Shayer: 'The Village Politicians'; signed; 40 by 35½ in; photograph by courtesy of M. Newman Ltd, London.

13 – William Shayer: 'A Farmstead: Milking Time'; signed; 53 by 44 in; photograph by courtesy of Tyne and Wear County Council Museums (Sunderland Art Gallery).

14 – William Shayer: 'Waiting for the Mackerel Boats'; signed and dated 1836; 28 by 36 in; photograph by courtesy of Richard Green Galleries, London.

15 – William Shayer: 'The Village Festival'; signed; 30 by 40 in; photograph by courtesy of Sotheby's.

16 – William Shayer: 'A Shady Corner'; originally signed and dated 1840; 28 by 36 in; courtesy of Southampton Art Gallery.

17 – William Shayer: 'The Village Festival' (also known as 'The Village Postman'); signed; 29½ by 39¼ in; photograph by courtesy of Richard Green Galleries, London.

18 – William Shayer: 'The Gipsy Encampment'; signed; 32½ by 39½ in; photograph by courtesy of Christie's.

19 – William Shayer: 'The Hampshire Farmer, Home Brew'd Ale'; 46 by 54 in; whereabouts now unknown. (See page 31.)

20 – William Shayer: 'Wash Day Companions'; signed;
24 by 20 in; photograph by courtesy of Richard Green
Galleries, London.

21 – William Shayer: 'Milking Time'; signed; 28 by 36 in; photograph by courtesy
of Southampton Art Gallery.

22 – William Shayer: 'Coast Scene, Isle of Wight'; signed and dated 1854; 25 by 39½ in; photograph by courtesy of Roger Freer Antiques, Northumberland.

23 – William Shayer: 'A Gypsy Encampment'; signed; 22 by 33 in; private collection.

24 – William Shayer: 'Rustics Playing Skittles outside the White Lion Inn'; signed; 28 by 36 in; photograph by courtesy of Arthur Ackermann and Son Ltd, London.

25 – William Shayer: 'Travellers Resting by the East Window of Netley Abbey'; signed; 30 by 40 in; photograph by courtesy of Christie's.

26 – William Shayer:
'Landscape with
Cattle by a Stream'
(also called 'Changing
Pastures'); signed;
28½ by 36¼ in;
photograph by
courtesy of City of
Manchester Art
Gallery.

27 – William Shayer:
'Fisherfolk on the
Shore'; signed and
dated 1855; 24 by 20
in; photograph by
courtesy of Christie's.

28 – William Shayer:
'Fisherfolk on the
Beach'; signed; 27½ by
35 in; photograph by
courtesy of Christie's.

29 – William Shayer:
'Wood Gatherer's
Repose'; signed; 27½ by
35½ in; photograph by
courtesy of M. Newman
Ltd, London.

30 – William Shayer: 'A Rocky Coastal Scene with Fisherfolk'; signed and dated 1851; 28 by 36 in; photograph by courtesy of the Leger Galleries Ltd, London.

31 – William Shayer: 'The Prawn Fishers'; signed; 24 by $29\frac{7}{8}$ in; photograph by courtesy of the Fitzwilliam Museum, Cambridge.

32 – William Shayer: 'Milking Time'; signed; on panel; 24 by 19½ in; photograph by courtesy of York Art Gallery.

33 – William Shayer: 'Cattle Watering'; signed; 29 by 39½ in; photograph by courtesy of Christie's.

34 – William Shayer:
'Travellers on a Path';
signed; 27 by 35 in;
photograph by courtesy
of Christie's.

35 – William Shayer:
'A Gypsy Girl selling
Jewellery'; signed; 33
by 48 in; photograph
by courtesy of
Christie's.

36 – William Shayer: 'Coast Scene with Figures'; signed; 31½ by 42 in; photograph by courtesy of Christie's.

37 – William Shayer: 'Fisherfolk on the Seashore'; signed and dated 1854; 28 by 36 in; photograph by courtesy of Christie's.

38 – William Shayer: 'Gypsies in the New Forest'; signed and dated '55; 40 by 33 in; photograph by courtesy of Frost and Reed Ltd, London.

39 – William Shayer: 'The Timber Waggon'; 40 by 33 in; photograph by courtesy of Leicester Museum and Art Gallery.

40 – William Shayer: 'A Young Girl Feeding a Grey Pony'; 20 by 24 in; photograph by courtesy of Richard Green Galleries, London.

42 – William Shayer: 'Travellers Outside the Blue Bell Inn'; signed; 28½ by 23½ in; photograph by courtesy of Sotheby's.

41 – William Shayer: 'Travellers Outside the Crown Inn'; signed and dated 1860; 29 by 24 in; photograph by courtesy of Richard Green Galleries, London. (See page 17.)

43 – William Shayer: 'Outside the Fisherman's Cottage'; signed; 40½ by 52½ in; photograph by courtesy of Cooling Galleries Ltd, London.

44 – William Shayer: 'A Cottage Interior'; signed; 17¾ by 23 in; panel; photograph by courtesy of Richard Green Galleries, London.

45 – William Shayer: 'A Gypsy Encampment'; signed and dated 1862; 17½ by 23½ in; private collection. (See letters by William Shayer on pages 35–37.)

46 – William Shayer:
'On the Beach, near
Southampton'; signed;
28 by 36 in;
photograph by courtesy
of the Leger Galleries
Ltd, London.

47 – William Shayer:
'The Plough Team';
signed; 27 by 36 in;
photograph by courtesy
of Christie's.

48 – William Shayer:
'Tired Pedlars'; signed;
24½ by 29 in;
photograph by courtesy
of Richard Green
Galleries, London.

49 – William Shayer:
'A Gypsy
Encampment'; signed;
27¾ by 36¼ in;
photograph by
courtesy of Oscar and
Peter Johnson Ltd,
London.

50 – William Shayer and Edward Charles Williams: 'A Halt outside the Bell Inn'; 30 by 50 in; photograph by courtesy of Christie's.

51 – William Joseph Shayer and Edward Charles Williams: 'The Old Half Way House'; signed; 30 by 50 in; photograph by courtesy of N. R. Omell Gallery, London.

52 – William Joseph Shayer: 'Match between T. Crosby's "Copper Captain" and Lord Lichfield's "Minster". October 1833'; signed and dated 1833; 16¾ by 21 in; on panel; photograph by courtesy of the National Trust, Anglesey Abbey, Cambridge.

53 – William Joseph Shayer: 'Hounds Starting a Hare in a Field of Turnips'; signed and dated 1836; 11½ by 15½ in; photograph by courtesy of Christie's.

54 – William Joseph Shayer: 'The Duke of Beaufort's Coach driven by the Marquess of Worcester' (see also colour plate); signed and dated 1840; $17\frac{3}{4}$ by $23\frac{1}{2}$ in; photograph by courtesy of Christie's.

55 – William Joseph Shayer: 'Coursing'; signed and dated 1842; $11\frac{3}{4}$ by 16 in; photograph by courtesy of Leicester Museum and Art Gallery.

56 – William Joseph Shayer: 'Two Bay Hunters'; signed and dated 1851; $47\frac{1}{2}$ by $59\frac{1}{2}$ in; photograph by courtesy of Richard Green Galleries, London.

57 – William Joseph Shayer: 'Hunting Scene' (one of a pair); signed and dated 1851; $13\frac{3}{4}$ by $17\frac{3}{4}$ in; photograph by courtesy of Arthur Ackermann and Son Ltd, London.

58 – William Joseph Shayer: 'A Wet Morning'; later engraved by J. Harris as one of a set of four; signed; 10 by 14 in; photograph by courtesy of Arthur Ackermann and Son Ltd, London.

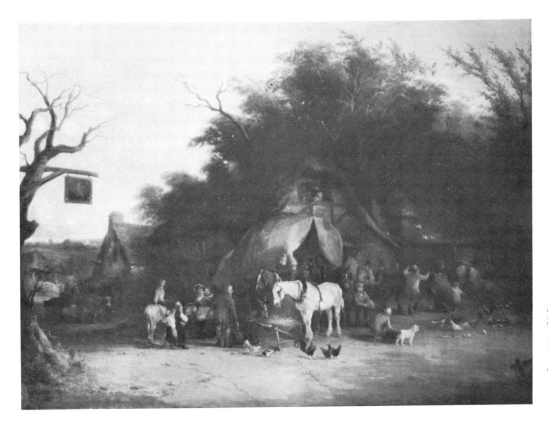

59 – William Joseph Shayer: 'Travellers Outside a Country Inn'; signed and dated 1858; $35\frac{3}{4}$ by $47\frac{3}{4}$ in; photograph by courtesy of Christie's.

60 – William Joseph Shayer: 'Mr Richard Sutton's "Lord Lyon"'; signed and dated 1866; 14 by 18 in; photograph by courtesy of Arthur Ackermann and Son Ltd, London.

61 – William Joseph Shayer: 'A Meet at the Crawley and Horsham Hunt'; signed and dated 1869; 24 by 36 in; photograph by courtesy of Arthur Ackermann and Son Ltd, London.

62 – William Joseph Shayer: 'Royal Mail Delivering at the Gate' (one of a pair); signed and dated 1863; 12 by 18 in; photograph by courtesy of Richard Green Galleries, London.

63 – William Joseph Shayer: 'The London–Southampton "Red Rover"'; bears J. F. Herring signature; 9½ by 12 in; private collection.

64 – William Joseph Shayer: 'The Brighton to Bristol "Red Rover" at a Crossroads' (one of a set of four, see also plates 65 and 66 and colour plate facing page 48); signed and dated 1878; 13 by 20 in; photograph by courtesy of Richard Green Galleries, London.

65 – William Joseph Shayer: 'The Guildford to London Coach Halted by a Hunt' (one of a set of four, see also plates 64 and 66 and colour plate facing page 48); signed and dated 1878; 13 by 20 in; photograph by courtesy of Richard Green Galleries, London.

66 – William Joseph Shayer: 'The London to Exeter Mail outside the Red Lion Inn' (one of a set of four, see also plates 64 and 65 and colour plate facing page 48); signed and dated 1878; 13 by 20 in; photograph by courtesy of Richard Green Galleries, London.

67 – William Joseph Shayer: 'Autumn: The Royal Mail Passing a Hunt Meet' (one of a set of four, see also plates 68, 69 and 70); signed and dated 1881; 13 by 21½ in; photograph by courtesy of Arthur Ackermann and Son Ltd, London.

68 – William Joseph Shayer: 'Winter: London–Newbury Stage Descending a Hill in the Snow' (one of a set of four, see also plates 67, 69 and 70); signed and dated 1881; 13 by 21½ in; photograph by courtesy of Arthur Ackermann and Son Ltd, London.

69 – William Joseph Shayer: 'Spring: London–Exeter Stage Taking Passengers' (one of a set of four, see also plates 67, 68 and 70); signed and dated 1881; 13 by $21\frac{1}{2}$ in; photograph by courtesy of Arthur Ackermann and Son Ltd, London.

70 – William Joseph Shayer: 'Summer: London–Andover Stage Climbing a Hill' (one of a set of four, see also plates 67, 68 and 69); signed and dated '81; 13 by $21\frac{1}{2}$ in; photograph by courtesy of Arthur Ackermann and Son Ltd, London.

71 – Henry Thring Shayer: 'The Traveller's Rest'; signed and dated 1850; 12¾ by 12 in; on board; photograph by courtesy of the Polak Gallery, London.

72 – Henry Thring Shayer: 'A Rural Scene'; signed; 14 by 17¾ in; photograph by courtesy of Oscar and Peter Johnson Ltd, London.

73 – Charles Waller Shayer: 'The Horse Fair'; signed; 26 by 44 in; photograph by courtesy of Walsall Museum and Art Gallery.

74 – Charles Waller Shayer: 'A Country Fair'; signed and dated 1875; 24 by 42 in; photograph by courtesy of M. Newman Ltd, London.

75 – Charles Waller Shayer: 'Drawing Cover'; signed; 17½ by 23½ in; on board; photograph by courtesy of Christie's.

76 – Henry and Charles Shayer: 'Sportsmen and Gundogs in a Wooded Landscape'; signed; 12 by 18 in; photograph by courtesy of Sotheby, King and Chasemore, Sussex.

77 – Henry and Charles Shayer: 'Coast Scene with Figures and Boats and a Church'; signed (also bears William Shayer's signature with the date 1833); $14\frac{1}{4}$ by 18 in; photograph by courtesy of Southampton Art Gallery.

78 – Henry and Charles Shayer: 'Landscape with Figures and Donkeys'; signed; 20 by 23 in; photograph by courtesy of Walsall Museum and Art Gallery.

79 – Henry and Charles
Shayer: 'Returning
Home' (one of a pair,
see plate 80); 6 by 8 in;
on millboard;
photograph by courtesy
of Oscar and Peter
Johnson Ltd, London.

80 – Henry and Charles
Shayer: 'The Watering
Place' (one of a pair,
see plate 79); 6 by 8 in;
on millboard;
photograph by
courtesy of Oscar and
Peter Johnson Ltd,
London.

81 – Henry and Charles
Shayer: 'On the
Common' (one of a
pair, see plate 82); 12
by 16 in; photograph
by courtesy of N. R.
Omell Gallery, London.

82 – Henry and Charles
Shayer: 'The Mid-Day
Rest' (one of a pair,
see plate 81); 12 by 16
in; photograph by
courtesy of N. R.
Omell Gallery, London.

83 – Henry and Charles Shayer: 'Hunting Scene – The Death'; signed; 26¼ by 45¼ in; photograph by courtesy of Arthur Ackermann and Son Ltd, London.

84 – Henry and Charles Shayer: 'The Meet' (one of a pair); signed; 26 by 45 in; photograph by courtesy of Christie's.

85 – Henry and Charles Shayer: 'The Ploughman's Midday Rest'; 36 by 60 in; photograph by courtesy of Richard Green Galleries, London.

86 – Henry and Charles Shayer: 'The End of a Day's Ploughing'; signed; 24 by 42 in; photograph by courtesy of Richard Green Galleries, London.

87 – Henry and Charles Shayer: 'The Gleaners' Midday Rest'; 40 by 50 in; photograph by courtesy of Frost and Reed Ltd, Bristol.

88 – Henry and Charles Shayer: 'Woodland River Landscape with Figure and Horses'; signed; 14 by 18 in; photograph by courtesy of Richard Green Galleries, London.

89 – Henry and Charles Shayer: 'A Wayside Chat'; 19½ by 29½ in; photograph by courtesy of Christie's.

90 – Henry and Charles Shayer: 'A Wooded Lane'; signed; 30 by 41½ in; photograph by courtesy of Christie's.

Index